Foreword by

CHRIS BRADY

MINDSET MEMOS

Bite-Sized Biographies for Learning to Think Like a Leader

OBSTACLÉS
PRESS

Life Leadership Essentials Series

First Edition, September 2016
10 9 8 7 6 5 4 3 2 1

Published by:

Obstaclés Press
200 Commonwealth Court
Cary, NC 27511

lifeleadership.com

ISBN 978-0-9976311-7-3

Library of Congress Control Number: 2016912479

Cover design and layout by Norm Williams, nwa-inc.com

Printed in the United States of America

CONTENTS

FOREWORD

by Chris Brady

I 've studied leaders for decades, and when considering their track records and actions, I'm always left pondering one particular question: "*How* did they *know* to do what they did?" It's one thing to read about the history of a country, company, or project and be told the facts about what happened. It's another to understand the why behind the what.

This was driven home to me while researching the development of the Kindle e-reader at Amazon, a story you will have the pleasure of reading in this book. As you will discover, Amazon founder Jeff Bezos was adamant that his vision of the future e-reader be carried out in a certain way. Particularly, he wanted seamless wireless connectivity to the internet at all times so that customers could buy a book directly from the device anytime, anywhere, without any hassle. There would be no rate plans, no ongoing subscriptions, and no download charges. This was all to avoid the need to hook the device up to a computer in order to purchase an e-book. Bezos' concept was that he should be able to hustle through an airport, remember that he had forgotten a book, and in seconds download one onto the reader without any technical knowledge or complication. It should be so easy a neophyte could do it with ease.

While this sounds logical, it was not easy to implement. For one thing, deals would have to be negotiated and struck between Amazon and wireless carriers all over the world. The costs could be astronomical. Further, no one had ever done anything like this before, and there could be no certainty it would work. Nearly everyone involved with Bezos on the project was opposed to this particular aspect of the reader, and many thought the risks far outweighed any of the potential gains in usability. But Bezos would not be moved and was insistent.

As I learned of Bezos' obstinacy in the face of opposition from his peers and subordinates, I was struck with my usual question: just how did he know this would be so important? Why did he insist on it even in the face of resistance from just about everyone on his team? Because in the end, of course, this one particular aspect of the Kindle design was the straw that broke the proverbial camel's back and brought the formerly resistant book publishers on board. Once Amazon representatives demonstrated to the publishers the easy connectivity that fostered spontaneous book buying, they were finally sold. It was the turning point in the whole, complicated, coordinated development project.

Had Bezos known this would turn out to be so important? After all, several years later the WhisperNet feature was quietly dropped from the Kindle with hardly a, well, whisper. But at the time it proved crucial to the

Kindle's success. We are left to conclude nothing other than the fact that Bezos could not have known specifically how important this feature would turn out to be, but conceptually he was convinced it was the right thing to do. And that is the key.

Great leaders never know for sure. They, after all, are leading people into waters in which they've never sailed themselves. That's the very picture of leadership. Many times the leader must lead others into places he himself has never been. At such times conviction is paramount. *Being right is not nearly as important as being sure.*

I could give several additional examples, as again and again I find this same dynamic when studying successful leaders. But this one is sufficient, because it so aptly demonstrates the concept. And here is my point: leaders don't know precisely what the future will bring, but they have a mindset that if they are not right about something, they will simply shift and end up making things right anyway. The goal is set, the vision is cast, and the leader is entirely committed to making it come true. Convictions come in strong, and they can sometimes be right, but they are also sometimes wrong. Ultimately, this doesn't even matter, because the greatest leaders have a mindset that regardless of the obstacle, they will get to their envisioned destination. The way is not as important as the reason for the journey in the first place. The path can change, but the vision remains.

It's a mindset. It's a passionate adherence to an inner compass. It's the response to a burning desire. And with the Kindle project, Bezos had it in spades. He would not be deterred. He knew intuitively what would be required to bring his vision to reality, and he would not be denied by the logic of those who would play it safe. If an obstacle were to pop up along the way (as they did in droves), he and his team could just pivot as necessary. But they kept their eye on the prize until it was realized.

That's the essence of the mindset of leadership. It can be expressed most clearly in the stories of what leaders do, which provide insight into *why* they did what they did.

In that spirit this book features several stories that are compelling for the leadership traits they display. The leaders are very diverse, ranging from business figures to artists and athletes, but the leadership lessons are a consistent thread running throughout. Read each carefully, and consider how the lessons involved apply to your own quest in life. Don't simply look at the *what*; seek to understand the deeper *why*. And there, in the reasons springing from the mindset of these great leaders, it is my hope you will find the conviction to pursue your own *why*.

Chris Brady
Cary, North Carolina

CHAPTER

1

TO LEAD THE WAY

*The manifest success of the Prius caused
a rethink on everybody's part.*

—BOB LUTZ, GENERAL MOTORS VICE CHAIRMAN, 2005

*I*n 2008, the Portland *Mercury* newspaper wrote the following: "You have a Prius, you probably compost, sort all your recycling and have a reusable shopping bag for your short drive to Whole Foods. You are the best. So do we really need the Obama sticker?"

There is no doubt the Toyota Prius hybrid car has become an icon for people who have a certain political alignment. There are a few cars that have become a symbol of a way of thinking or a political statement. Another great example would be the Volkswagen bug and its ugly stepbrother, the van. If you happen to have been alive during the era of "flower power," you probably know what I mean. A pickup truck is another example. There is a certain image of a person who drives a Ford F-150, and it's probably not that of an attorney. The Mercedes-Benz has always been a status symbol, a way to show the world that you have "made it" financially. Then you have the Jeep Wrangler, which is for the truly cool and fun-loving people.

There's a fascinating story about how the Toyota Prius got to be this icon type of car—and about how it even came to be made at all. Whatever your opinion of the car, you have to respect that it is something different that was brought to the market in a big and effective way. It's been a huge success.

As a hybrid, the Prius runs on two different modes of propulsion: electric and gasoline. The gasoline engine powers up the electric side, which propels the car when the gasoline engine isn't needed. It's called a parallel system hybrid because it runs back and forth between gas and electric. It was one of the first of its kind.

However, the hybrid idea is not new. In the 1830s a Scottish inventor built a crude electric vehicle, though it wouldn't go very far. In the early 1900s, a young German man developed a crude hybrid car that used a gasoline engine to spin an electric generator that made the car go, fairly close to the workings of the Prius. The German inventor's name, by the way, was Ferdinand Porsche.

More attempts at electric or partially electric vehicles arose through the century, many of them in the early 1900s. The 1950s brought us golf carts, which are electric but aren't exactly cars. In the sixties, engineers at TRW conjured up a hodgepodge hybrid with a Beetle engine, a Westinghouse electric generator, a DC motor from GE, and a Chrysler transmission. They put that whole drive system into the body of a 1962 Pontiac Tempest and called it the

EM for "electromechanical transmission." This attempt to increase fuel economy was just too expensive and way ahead of its time. With gas at twenty-four cents a gallon, people just weren't that interested in economy at the time.

General Motors took a stab at the electric car in the nineties, which they sold as the EV1. It was an odd-looking car, and it had a limited range of one hundred miles. The EV1 had trouble with engine fires, which left some bad impressions with consumers, and you could only lease the cars, since for some reason GM wanted the batteries back in the end. When they discontinued the model, they called all the cars back in. One actress in Hollywood loved hers and tried to sue in order to keep it, but she lost, and the car was destroyed with the rest. In 2007, *Time* magazine named the EV1 one of the worst cars of all time.

In 1993 the government got involved by sponsoring an organization called the Partnership for a New Generation of Vehicles (PNGV). It included eight federal agencies, several universities, and Detroit's big three car companies. In bureaucratic style, the PNGV accomplished little, but it did create what turned out to be an important situation. Other carmakers, such as Toyota, were upset by not being included in the PNGV. As a result, Toyota decided that they could produce an alternative fuel vehicle of their own. This led to a most interesting and unusual story.

Takeshi Uchiyamada is the unlikely hero of this tale. He was just a normal guy who grew up in Toyota city and went to college locally in Japan. Toyota City is dominated, of course, by Toyota Motor Company and all of its suppliers.

Uchiyamada went to college locally, studying physics, and went to work at the only game in town. He had always dreamed of leading a vehicle development team—the most exciting and creative job in the auto industry. Uchiyamada, however, was stuck doing things like sound-proofing development—working with foam and padding to make cars quieter.

Slowly, and without much flash, he worked his way up Toyota's bureaucracy. In 1993, he was the surprise choice to run the department called the Vehicle Development Center Number Two. One can almost see him going home and taking his wife out to dinner to celebrate. "We've made the big-time, babe. Vehicle Development Center Number Two. It's all mine."

His task was to lead a team in developing Toyota's flagship family-sized car but with better fuel efficiency and emissions. Everyone involved at the time thought it would be another larger car, like a Corolla on steroids with better technology. Essentially, they expected a car including some innovation, but just an advanced version of what they already had.

Author Paul Ingrassia wrote, "Uchiyamada was an unconventional choice to lead this effort, but that was just the point. His bosses believed that his lack of experience on a vehicle development team would make him less likely to be bound by conventional wisdom."[1] In other words, they wanted someone who didn't consider himself to be an expert because they wanted to maximize innovation and creativity. They wanted someone who didn't know what he didn't know, who might make mistakes that could lead to something productive.

Often it's the naïve who drive innovation—those who don't know they aren't supposed to succeed. If you take many of the most innovative companies, like Apple or Google for instance, you will find there were experts and analysts lined up to tell them they wouldn't, couldn't, and shouldn't succeed. But these companies just didn't know any better.

> OFTEN IT'S THE NAÏVE WHO DRIVE INNOVATION—THOSE WHO DON'T KNOW THEY AREN'T SUPPOSED TO SUCCEED.

Toyota Motor Company was wise enough to recognize the power of naiveté, and they took a competent mid-level technical manager and put him in charge of a project they hoped would be innovative. The project was called G21, which stood for Global 21st Century. Uchiyamada and his team began developing a car that could best be described as a *directional innovation*.

In a move designed to impress their bosses, the G21 team developed a concept car using hybrid technology, with the goal of displaying it at the 1995 Tokyo Motor Show. It actually wasn't even quite a car because it couldn't yet propel itself. You couldn't actually drive it. They brought it in on dollies, plopped it there in the middle of the auto show, and said, "It's a hybrid." It had some hybrid technology, of course, but it was a concept car, an idea of a car that *could be*.

The bosses liked the concept car so much they decided it should be developed for mass production and that its development should take the place of the car that Uchiyamada's team was originally pursuing. The name they gave the new car was *Prius*, which is Latin for "to go before" or "to lead the way." They wanted a forward-looking car to go with the forward-looking name. The catch, and the problem to be solved, was that Toyota's goal for this car was 50 percent better fuel economy than the Corolla and significantly less emissions. The Corolla was already an efficient car — it didn't guzzle gas. To top it by 50 percent would be quite a task.

Uchiyamada knew that this was an outrageous goal, and his bosses might have agreed with him. Nevertheless, they told him he would lose his position at the head of the project team if he didn't agree to do it. So, like a good soldier, he decided to give it a go. They went through more than eighty different hybrid design attempts, trying to come up with something that would actually work. Nothing really did.

Then a new president took over at Toyota, Hiroshi Okuda. He was the first "outsider" to become president of the company in thirty years. His idea was that Toyota as a company had become fat and slow. Uchiyamada had figured that if they went full throttle, the Prius might be ready by 1999. But this timetable was too slow for the incoming president. He instead wanted the release to coincide with the United Nations Conference on Climate Change that was to be held in nearby Kyoto in 1997!

Once again Uchiyamada and everyone involved knew this was outrageous. The 1999 goal had already been aggressive. Everyone in the industry knows it takes three to four years to develop a normal car, but a significantly innovative car is a different matter. As it was a whole new platform, many technological advances were required. The task was more than unlikely — it was *impossible*.

Nevertheless, they went to it and began working sixteen-hour days, seven days a week. Most of the team moved their living quarters right onto the premises. In Toyota City they have dormitory rooms available on a short-term rent basis, so during such big projects workers can just go flop and sleep for a few hours and not have to actually leave work. The Prius team took this to a higher level by making it a long-term arrangement, more or less.

Uchiyamada said, in effect, "I couldn't just go to my people and say, 'Management's crazy. This new jerk that runs the place has no idea how to make a car. He's from the outside. His expectations are ridiculous. We'll never make it, but let's give it the old college try.'"

> "I HAD TO GET MYSELF TO WHERE I COULD BELIEVE THAT IT COULD BE DONE, AND ONCE I COULD GET TO WHERE I COULD BELIEVE IT COULD BE DONE, THEN I KNEW I COULD GET THEM TO BELIEVE IT COULD BE DONE."
> —TAKESHI UCHIYAMADA

He couldn't do that and hope to succeed. That's not real leadership.

He said, "I had to get myself to where I could believe that it could be done, and once I could get to where I could believe it could be done, then I knew I could get them to believe it could be done." He added, "Only then I thought maybe we'd have a 5 percent chance."

To get inspiration, Uchiyamada sought out other times when such impossible tasks with impossible deadlines were achieved. There were two in particular that he studied. One was the development of the Kushu J7W1 Shinden, which was the jet fighter plane Japanese engineers developed in less than one year near the end of the Second World War. The other one was John F. Kennedy's goal of putting a man on the moon in under a decade. The moon landing actually happened in much less time than that, even though at the time Kennedy said it, the technology needed to accomplish that goal didn't even exist.

Uchiyamada's reading and study brought him to adopt a project-management system used by NASA. At one point, the G21 team's main test car wouldn't run, and they couldn't figure out why. They had, by this point, unlimited access to the resources of Toyota's design, engineering, and development staffs. He could choose anybody, throw any resources at it—it was a fire drill in which anything goes. The team got the best of the best within Toyota, and that is saying something. Still, no one could figure out what was wrong with the test car. Everything seemed to be right, but it just wouldn't propel itself.

For fifty-nine days, around the clock, the best minds at Toyota worked on figuring out the problem. It might be important, for instance, for a new car to actually move! Eventually, they figured it out and got back on track.

The project was not completed without tragedy, however. Since batteries sometimes function poorly in the cold and at high elevation, engineers performed cold weather tests on the Prius in one of the coldest places in Japan: Mount Fuji. Eight people involved in that testing boarded a helicopter that flew them off the mountain. Sadly, the helicopter crashed. The eight were lost, including the lead cold weather engineer for the project.

Another challenge was the many new technologies that needed to be developed and then integrated into the car. The team was filing patents and coming up with new ideas and inventions almost monthly.

All of these challenges were overcome, though, and the Prius was indeed unveiled in October of 1997 in Tokyo, on time. Toyota's calculation was that the car would go sixty-six miles on one gallon of gas, which was double the Corolla's performance at the time. That might have been a bit optimistic, regulators later said, but the Prius had phenomenal fuel economy at any rate.

When they launched the Prius in the United States, however, there were some troubles. First of all, the car was slow. Second, it was expensive compared to other cars its size. Finally, it was simply strange! It had an odd interior with features placed in unlikely places. Perhaps a bit too much creativity had been employed in designing the interior ergonomics.

There was competition as well. Honda upstaged Toyota by releasing the Insight in the United States. The Insight was a gas-electric hybrid as well, but more of a gimmick, and as it turned out not to work well or sell well.

Toyota was up to the challenge, however, and they persisted and innovated to get the car firmly into the American market. One thing they did that had never been done before was to offer a web page where customers could actually purchase the car, right online. They also allowed people to take them on month-long test drives. Further, it was decided that movie stars would be likely to take to the environmentally friendly car first, and Toyota targeted them for early adoption of the hybrid technology. These stars would show up at the big award ceremonies where usually limos and Hummers were the rule, but suddenly there would be a line of little Priuses. People noticed, and it caused a stir. It was Arnold Schwarzenegger in one of his seven Hummers versus George Clooney in his Prius. Tech legend Steve Wozniak was famous for having one of each, a Hummer and a Prius. The Hollywood star/famous names strategy worked, and the car received a ton of visibility leading into its official launch.

When the day came that the Prius was to go on sale and the online store was to begin actually selling the car, no one really knew if anyone would buy it. The salespeople in the United States gathered around their terminals to see if anyone would click the "buy" button. They had no idea if it would work because no one had ever done this before.

They needn't have worried; more cars sold in that first hour than were expected to in a month. As a result, the Toyota sales team got a little swept away with their exuberance. They decided to run all kinds of fun and quirky promotions. For one, anyone who bought a Prius in those early days would be mailed decals for the back of their car. One read, "Eat my voltage." Another said, "Up your wattage." Yet another, "Kiss my current." Some of the brass back in Japan found out about this and grew concerned about the company image. The expressions on the decals didn't translate into Japanese very well, so Toyota actually did a recall of the window decals. This was probably the first and only time in automotive history that there was a recall on stickers.

As Paul Ingrassia wrote, "Toyota had launched the first practical mass-market hybrid car in the world's largest automotive market, and it had done so right under the nose of Detroit, then too busy counting its profits from selling SUVs."[2] The Prius first took root among what one author called the "Granola-fed dilletantes flaunting their Priuses as signs of moral superiority."[3]

But eventually the Prius's popularity spread to people who also wanted to save money. A better version of the car was released in 2004. The claim was that the typical driver could save about $350 a month on fuel costs. For many people, that was enough savings to justify the extra cost of the car, and it turned out to be a real value proposition for the customer.

Today, there are plenty of copies and "me-toos" from different car manufacturers, and we've even seen the dawn of the fully functional all-electric car in the form of the wonderful Tesla. But no matter whatever happens with the alternative-propulsion vehicle market, the Prius will always be the most famous as the flagship, the one that completely ushered in the era. Uchiyamada and his frantic team had brought on a new phase in automotive history, not only creating an iconic car, but also forever changing consumer perception about automotive propulsion.

This story is inspiring. One can envision Mr. Uchiyamada and his unnamed team working tremendously long hours, doing something everybody said couldn't be done. They achieved what other people trying over the previous hundred years could not. To apply the meaning of the word *Prius*, we too can "lead the way." There are many applications that can be drawn from this story that apply to our own lives, businesses, careers, and endeavors.

MINDSET MEMOS

1. Inauspicious beginnings do not preclude marvelous success.

To use plain English: Just because it looks ugly in the beginning doesn't mean it can't or won't turn out beautiful in the end. Many endeavors that don't seem to be working in the beginning turn out to be absolutely marvelous.

2. Just because something has been attempted many times before without success doesn't mean you won't succeed.

In truth, if every aspiring leader and innovator were to listen to the people who say something can't be done, probably nothing *would* be done.

If you're going to lead in any category in life, one of the most important things to know is that the critics are wrong. Sometimes proving them wrong can be the most exciting sporting event you'll ever take part in.

3. Solutions put forward by bureaucrats and politicians rarely work.

It is private enterprise that innovates. Businesses aren't just about making a profit. They create wonderful products that can change things for the better. The government agency that was formed to create an alternatively fueled vehicle produced nothing.

It's rare when bureaucrats out-innovate entrepreneurs. But it's common for entrepreneurs to out-innovate the government. The Wright brothers outdid all those who were given government grants to build an airplane, for instance. A couple of independent bicycle manufacturers out of Ohio beat all the bureaucrats and government-funded airplane enterprises to the punch. While the government agency floundered, Uchiyamada, a leader who inspired his team, who found reasons to believe they could do it, stepped in and made it happen.

4. Sometimes something you do as a "side" turns into your life's major calling.

We need to have our eyes open to possibilities that don't necessarily look neat and tidy or straight and linear when they come along. Don't miss what could happen from a beautiful "side" project.

5. Setting an outrageous goal is sometimes a ridiculously good strategy.
As Chris Brady stated, "The secret to great accomplishment is setting an unbelievable, almost ridiculous goal and having not quite enough time to hit it."

6. Timing is often critical to success.
Toyota realized that the international conference on global climate change was taking place right down the road in their own country and that they would have the eyes of the world on them. This was the perfect stage set for a car that would help the environment, and that fact drove an entire corporation to throw its resources into something that had never successfully been done before. The timing was tight and pressure-packed, but it was also magnificent.

7. We can gain belief and inspiration by looking at other examples of success.
It doesn't matter where it is, what category it happens in, or who did it — excellence is instructive. When we look at a situation in which someone has succeeded remarkably at something, we should think, "I'd like

to know more about what happened there. "Success never proceeds like this: "They came out with a car which was instantly successful. They are all geniuses and were perfect, and there were no troubles in development, and everyone saw it working all along." It's always the opposite. "They never thought it would work. They were laughed at, spit upon, ridiculed, and ostracized. They weren't qualified and didn't have the right degrees."

Usually the people involved in these moon shots are scared to death. They are the knuckleheads. Then you follow the story backward from massive success to the knuckleheads, and you think, "I'm not that bad, not that clueless. I am ahead of where they started. If they succeeded, what could happen with me?" That is exactly the point.

8. Reading is powerful.

Uchiyamada turned to reading to give himself belief, so that he could then in turn give his team belief. Reading is much more than entertainment. It fosters inspiration, understanding, greatness, and hope.

9. It might not be important how or where you start, but how you finish is critical.

This isn't just referring to actually finishing the race or the project. It also refers to how you put the finishing touches on what you do. People will often go a long way toward success but then skimp at the end and not do the work to put the finishing touches on what they've done. Uchiyamada and his team of engineers successfully punched through all the barriers technologically, but without the finishing touches, who knows if they would have been successful? Without the elegance in the rollout, the innovative promotion, and the excellent timing, maybe the Prius wouldn't have become the iconic car that it is.

Uchiyamada and his team put the finish on the finish, however, and they ushered in a new era in automotive propulsion. Often, when you think you are done, you're not completely done. Any time something truly excellent takes place, it's that last little bit that makes all the difference. It's the slight-edge principle. Most of your gain and benefit will come from that little extra bit you put in at the end.

10. There will always be competition.
Even if the competition is half-baked, as in this case, it will be there. Be ready to push through and to innovate to compete. Someone will always be breathing down your neck.

11. Innovation applies to all facets of endeavor.
Innovation is not just a technology thing. Anything you do in your career, your business, or your

profession can benefit from innovation. Look for ways to make it better, more excellent. Be clever. Never stop.

12. Know your market.

Toyota didn't market the Prius to deer hunters, bodybuilders, or hot-rodders who like to drag race on Saturday night. Your market is never *everyone*. Sometimes, as with the Prius, you have to go big by going narrow. Clearly define your target, and hit it with precision.

13. Have fun.

Don't be afraid to have fun and even to make some mistakes while you're having fun. "Kiss my current."

14. Keep improving your product.

Provide real value for real people. The 2004 version of the Prius was much improved, much more intuitive, and more designed for the average person who was as concerned about saving money as about saving the planet. A car that began as innovative quickly evolved to being revolutionary. Remember, your masterpiece is really just your first version. Are you proud of what you've done? Great. Get busy improving it even further. Iterate relentlessly

CHAPTER

2

KISS AND MAKE UP

We're hitting places they've never seen a big band, and they'll remember us forever.

—Gene Simmons

Stanley Eisen, age eighteen, and Gene Klein, age twenty-one, were introduced to each other in 1970. A mutual friend thought they might work well together. But they didn't immediately hit it off. Both were bright, ambitious, hardworking, clean, and sober types. Both had grown up in Queens and were of Jewish descent. They didn't really care for one another at first, but they had so much in common it just made sense for them to work together.

Gene said, "I came from another country. I didn't have brothers and sisters to depend on. My mother lived through the Nazi German concentration camps of World War II. Early on my father left us. I had no support system and my mom was working from dawn 'til dusk. There are no excuses. You're going to go somewhere if you pick yourself up off the ground and make things happen."[4]

With similar mindsets, the two became a team. They formed a band with a few other guys and named themselves Rainbow. Later, they changed the name to Wicked Lester. That's marketing genius right there.

They had ambition, and they had a band, but they hadn't quite struck the right chord just yet. They started working with a local recording studio called Electric Lady Studios. Gene and Stan were able to get in as session musicians, playing backup guitar and backup vocals for other bands and acts to earn a little money. More important, though, was the valuable experience and inside knowledge they were gaining of the music business. Gene said, "We were practically living at Electric Lady Studios. For us, it was like the school of hard knocks. It really opened our eyes to a new world, a world we wanted to be a part of." Stan added, "It was a great education."[5]

The two bandmates decided to make a gutsy move. They had a record deal with Epic Records with their Wicked Lester band but knew that band would never get them where their ever-growing vision was taking them. So they broke up the band and cancelled their record contract. Gene explained, "Wicked Lester lacked a definitive sound and identity." Stan added, "The band wasn't going anywhere, so why labor over something that's flawed from the start?"[6]

It was a true swing-for-the-bleachers move. Gene said, "I honestly can't explain why we had that clarity and vision because most people wouldn't look a gift horse in the mouth. We had a recording contract, we finished an album with a major label. You have to be arrogant, delusional, or insane to walk away from a record deal."[7] But that's exactly what they did.

Gene and Stan realized they couldn't let good hold them back from great, and they believed they were destined for greatness. They weren't interested in just making some money or in simply "doing well." They both had a driving vision that went way beyond any of that.

They found day jobs to get by while they planned their next enterprise. Gene became a Dictaphone typist at the Puerto Rican Interagency Council. Stan worked at a sandwich shop by day and drove cabs by night. When they weren't working their jobs, they set about clearly defining their music, aiming for a specific signature sound. Defining who they wanted to be as musicians was their number-one priority. "We wanted a band that had heavy guitars," Stan said, "but songs with strong melodies and choruses."[8] They studied a wide range of bands. In particular, they liked a lot of the British bands that had come onto the scene in the early seventies.

"We realized that the bands we loved not only put out great music, but they delivered live," Gene said. "They were fun to see in concert." Stan took it even further and said, "We wanted to be the band we never saw on stage."[9] They recognized that stage presence was a key element, but there seemed to be room for more, something that no one had done yet. They believed they could provide that extra something.

The duo picked up a drummer in the fall of 1972 from an ad placed in *Rolling Stone* magazine. The trio honed their skills daily in a dilapidated loft above a bar. "We rehearsed constantly," Stan recalls. They had no contract or prospects and they were working hard at their day jobs to pay the bills. The band auditioned for several record labels, halfheartedly still using the Wicked Lester name, but was rejected every time.

They thought they would be a power trio, like The Who or the Jimi Hendrix Experience, but it became apparent that there was a missing element. A lead guitar might provide a bit more melody and style. Klein and Eisen put an ad in the paper, "Lead guitarist wanted with flash and ability. Album out shortly." (That last part was, of course, wishful thinking.) The ad ended with a great phrase: "No time-wasters please." They weren't messing around. Their vision was to make it big time.

Nearly sixty guys auditioned, and almost everybody was wrong for the part. One guy came in with a Spanish guitar and a sombrero. Another could barely play, but thought if he just wore the right clothes, he'd get hired. It was terrible.

Then another guy showed up, an alcoholic who was driven to the audition by his mother. He was making all sorts of rude noises when one of the other guys was auditioning. But when he started to play, Gene and Stan knew immediately he was their guy. He could rip out the melodious hard-rock lead riffs that were exactly what the band was looking for.

"I always felt I had something," the newcomer later said. "I used to tell my girlfriend that I was gonna be a millionaire and famous. They always used to laugh at me. Everybody did. Even all my friends." Said Stan of the new guy, "He...belonged in the band. He was the missing piece, the missing link. It just now all gelled, now made sense."[10]

They gelled into the hard rock band we now know as KISS. Stanley Eisen started to use the name Paul Stanley, Gene Klein started to go by Gene Simmons, the drummer was Peter Criss, and the last addition was the great Ace Frehley. They would go on to become household names, but at the beginning they were just four guys with lots of ideas about what would make a great rock band. Peter Criss said, "We copied a lot of things. A lot of our ideas. The art of what we did came from the Beatles, Alice Cooper, and the New York Dolls. We sat down and said, 'What if all this was rolled into one?' And it worked. It was brilliant."[11]

Through all this, Gene and Paul were the leaders, the visionaries, the businessmen and driving force for the band. They were determined and committed. Peter and Ace brought the rock-and-roll looseness, the artistic flair that made it work—and unfortunately, the substance abuse as well. But they all came together as a team. Each individual had a specific role, and it worked well. It was the power of a team coming together.

KISS was definitely not an overnight success, however. Their first show was at a seedy little joint in Queens called the Coventry. Outside of their girlfriends, brothers and sisters, and their moms and dads, there were precisely six people there.

They played as one of five bands on a bill so that the fans of the other bands might see the act, and they would slowly pick up a fan here and one there. Gene Simmons started calling clubs and selling like mad to get gigs. He said, "I've been a salesman my entire life."

Even with the humble start, they thought big, imagining themselves as an international act. Gene said, "Like the Beatles, we wanted to have a band where you had four distinct individuals. You could be a fan of the band and a fan of a different persona as well."[12]

These guys deliberately, intentionally, thoughtfully designed their image and their brand. They said, "We started wearing makeup when Alice Cooper took his off, when David Bowie left it, and when Genesis thought it was no longer cool to wear it."[13] Just at the point where the glamour makeup trend had started to wear thin, KISS resurrected it and did it to the max. Their idea was not just a little white with some rouge, but they created whole characters they could become on stage. One was the rock star lover, another was the mean monster, another was a spaceman, and the final character was a cat. For a time no one even knew their actual identities, which only added to their mystique.

They played with the same intensity no matter how many people were present. Paul Stanley said, "Whether there were four people or 40,000, it didn't matter. Our path was already predetermined. I was completely oblivious to anything, other than we were gonna be the biggest band around."[14] Picture these four young guys as if you did not know the rest of the story. They were playing their hearts out, dressed up in a way no one had ever seen, and plenty of people thought they were just nuts. Alice Cooper, no stranger to on-stage shenanigans, saw their act and sarcastically remarked, "I think the thing they need is a gimmick."[15]

Everyone they worked with in those early days mentioned two things: one was how professional they were, and the other was their determination. Clubs wanted them to play top-forty hits, but they refused. They insisted on playing only their original stuff. Once they had their look and their sound down, they stuck to their brand. This allowed them to play at only a couple of places, so they just played there all the time, looking for traction, building up a following.

KISS had invented their own category, and they had the guts to be outrageous when most people would have been flat-out embarrassed. They innovated like crazy, always improving on the gimmick. A monster, apparently, should spit blood, so they figured out a way to have the monster character spit blood. Somebody suggested they do some fire breathing, but nobody in the band wanted to. Gene Simmons finally volunteered, and he would drink this kerosene mouthwash and blow on a cotton swab attached to the end of a post, causing concern with venues and fire marshals. They were intimidating as it was. All four of them were fairly tall, and when you added the platform boots and the crazy costumes, it had quite the effect on people. Now mix in spitting blood and breathing fire!

One of the keys to their eventual success was that they continued rehearsing seven days a week, and they scripted everything. They had certain parts in certain songs when the guitarists would stand next to each other and go through choreographed moves, which they would make look spontaneous. They worked hard to ensure each element was scripted into the show for maximum effect.

In the early days, in a situation that probably demonstrates their determination more than anything, they played a fund-raiser for the Palisades Free Library at the Lamont-Doherty Earth Observatory. Just imagine the type of individual who, in your mind, supports a library, and then picture KISS. One can envision a woman in her sixties who likes to read, maybe has a chain on her glasses and a couple of cute grandkid photos on the refrigerator, going to this fund-raiser for a library in formal attire. Perhaps her husband is in his tux, and they are used to doing this. They go every year and see jazz musicians and string quartets, but this particular year goes a little differently!

The benefit was set up in a large tent next to a hall overlooking the Hudson River in a quiet neighborhood. KISS, before getting into their makeup, showed up and mingled with the crowd. They helped set up chairs and spread the tablecloths before it started. They danced with some of the older ladies as the string quartet played. Then they went down the road to their friends' house, sat down in his kitchen, and put on their makeup, monster suits, and the works.

KISS did their full concert, full volume—fire, blood, everything. It was so loud the neighborhood kids could hear it, and they of course came running to see what was going on. Nothing like that had ever happened at the Observatory before. The crowd swelled to almost three hundred people—the biggest crowd KISS had ever played for up to that time.

Early the next morning, the band showed up in street clothes to help clean up all the debris and the chairs and stack everything. They did the whole show for free, just for the exposure. Paul said, "The belief was always that there will be great memories in part of the building blocks of what we were doing."[16] They were willing to do anything. They would walk into situations which were the wrong setting, the wrong venue, the wrong audience, everything, and play their hearts out anyway. Anything they could do to make it, to play one more gig and get exposure, they would do.

KISS eventually got a record contract with a struggling label called Casablanca Records. They put out three albums but couldn't get any radio play. No one would take them seriously. They toured all over North America, realizing their secret sauce was their live show. Most people would spend the first few minutes of a KISS show simply startled and bewildered. But by the end of the show, if they stuck around, they were converted, if at least just by the spectacle.

They called it the "dartboard tour" because they would take a gig anywhere they could get it, without any planning of routes or a logical travel schedule. Their albums weren't selling, their record label was broke, and the band was broke. They had an expensive and elaborate set and a whole bunch of semitrucks and roadies to pay. One night they would be in Toronto, the next Columbus, Ohio, and then the next night in Memphis. Two or three days later they'd need to be in Calgary, and then back to Toronto. At one point they were so desperate for money that Paul and Gene sang on an AMC Truck commercial. Another time they had to stay with a couple of the roadies because their credit card was declined. Among six of them they had two dollars to make it through a weekend.

Finally, their managers and the record label made a strategic decision. They realized they would have to target a specific, narrow market where the band's sound would resonate with the youth of that area. They needed a place where they could build a solid fan base, apply a concentration of force, and then launch from there. That market and place happened to be southern Michigan.

Their reasoning was that the people who worked in the auto industry tended to like loud, hard-core music that could be heard over the noise at their workbench in the factory. Because these shop workers would listen at work, they reasoned, they wouldn't mind their teenagers listening to it. Alice Cooper and Bob Seeger had made it big there on similar reasoning. So KISS made a last-ditch effort with their remaining money in southern Michigan.

Not many people pull southern Michigan out of their hat as their key strategy, but for KISS, it became the turning point.

In Cadillac, Michigan, in 1974, the high school football team lost their first two games in the fall. Jim Neff, a young assistant coach, had the thought that if they brought a record player into the locker room, it would help fire up the boys. The tight-laced ex-Marine head coach wasn't so sure, but nothing else was working, so he let Neff do it. Neff just happened to have picked a KISS album, which is amazing because they had sold so few of them. His strategy worked. The football team got fired up and went on to win a bunch of games in a row. It must be the rock and roll, Neff figured.

Neff turned over the KISS album, and on the back there was an address and phone number, which he called. Eventually he reached Gene Simmons himself. He told Gene the story, and Gene asked him to call him every week and report how the team had done after getting fired up by the KISS music. Eventually, Gene supplied the coach with free tickets to come see the band play at COBO Hall in Detroit. Neff noticed that KISS was scheduled to return the next year at the same venue, so he asked if the band would come and participate in the school's homecoming parade and give a concert in the school gym. Of course, KISS agreed. They'd played lesser, gigs, after all—like library fund-raisers!

They showed up at the high school the next year in their full monster costume getup, marched out onto the field with the cheerleaders and color guard, and then sat on a float driving through downtown Cadillac, Michigan, throwing Hershey Kisses to the kids. Elementary kids were invited, and the teachers let each one have his or her face painted like their favorite KISS character. There are pictures of the KISS guys in front of the bleachers and five- to seven-year-old boys and girls all dressed up like KISS. Gene Simmons is lying on the floor with his arm around a little girl, and Paul Stanley is bouncing a little boy on his knee. Some things you just can't make up.

The school wouldn't allow the blood spitting or fire breathing, but the band still said it was one of their craziest concerts ever. All the kids in the audience had their faces painted like KISS, and the band had a surreal experience looking out at the 3,000 faces, painted just like their own, looking back at them.

KISS had tried hard to make it into the mainstream. They had attempted to get *Rolling Stone* magazine to do an article on them, to no avail. They couldn't get in the papers or on the radio or get their albums to sell. They had hung out in full KISS regalia in malls and stationed themselves at record stores signing albums and promoting the band but with little success. They just couldn't seem to break through. Try as they might, nothing had really worked to break them through to the next level.

At that event at Cadillac High School in southern Michigan, suddenly they made international news. Monsters hugging children—it was just too crazy to ignore. KISS even paid the city for the extra costs of the whole affair. They surprised the kids by arranging for a Huey helicopter to fly over the lake and land there in the middle of the field, and the four KISS guys got in and flew away, hanging out of the open doors waving.

Publicist Carol Ross said, "The Cadillac High event was the breakthrough for the mainstream press…. An event born of a willingness to serve gave them the break they'd been working so hard for, for so many years. Then, the KISS Alive album came out next, capturing their real strength, the real sound, what people actually liked about them, the live concert experience, and they were off to the races."[17]

> "AN EVENT BORN OF A WILLINGNESS TO SERVE GAVE THEM THE BREAK THEY'D BEEN WORKING SO HARD FOR, FOR SO MANY YEARS."
> —CAROL ROSS

Fin Costello, the photographer for that KISS Alive album, said, "KISS understood American culture and they understood the potential of what they were doing. They rose to every occasion. They weren't playing stars. As celebrity culture developed over the ensuing years, anybody who was successful became distanced from their audience very quickly. That wasn't happening with KISS. They were just part of the crowd, chatting away to everyone. The final ingredient in them making it was humility and a willingness to serve."[18]

There is much more to this story, of course. We could talk about the genius of the merchandising empire they built up over the years and the hundreds of millions of dollars they made. We could talk about the sold-out arenas they played to all over the world. We could talk about the KISS Army Fan Club, which is one of first rock-and-roll fan clubs. There is a lot more, good and bad, but this early story of how four humble, determined, creative guys made it into the big time holds some amazing lessons that we can apply to our lives.

MINDSET MEMOS

1. Find a definite identity, and focus on what you want to be.

In your professional life, in your company, in your business, and even personally, this likely applies. Have a definite idea about what you want to become, and work hard on that identity. Define it intentionally.

2. Put yourself in a market of one.

Be the only one doing what you are doing. The best way to do that is by forming new combinations. Fiery rock and stylish theatricality might be the two components that KISS blended the best. These two things existed before, but no one had ever put them together close to the same way they did. What is the combination that could set you apart as a true original?

3. You must have not only the right product but the right way to market it as well.

You can have great ideas, but having a great idea alone doesn't make the idea work. Great ideas always live or die in the implementation phase.

4. Be publicity and media savvy.

In today's world, you need to understand how to work the media in order to amplify, define, and control your message.

5. Know your target market.

Know it and build a following by consciously serving that market over and over again. Eventually, KISS realized their live show was their secret sauce, and so they kept playing to their strength over and over again until it opened doors for them to finally break out.

6. Have the guts to swing for the bleachers.

When Gene and Paul broke up their original band, Wicked Lester, they took a huge risk. They did it because they knew it wasn't what they wanted long term. It couldn't get them where they wanted to go. It wasn't quite right, and they weren't willing to settle for good when great was available, even though there was no guarantee that great *was* available. They swung for the bleachers anyway.

7. Go for excellence, even if it means huge costs.

Even if it means most of the clubs won't let you play there because you refuse to do somebody else's agenda, stick to your guns. You can't get stuck playing top-forty hits. You have to play your original stuff, or you'll never break out. You don't want to be a cover band.

KISS went for excellence, even when it meant huge costs. They went for excellence even when it meant being broke for years and maybe never even making it big. They never compromised.

8. Define, learn, do.

Define where you want to be first very clearly, specifically, and precisely. Learn from people who have done those things, and then get busy doing exactly those things. KISS studied David Bowie, Alice Cooper, the Beatles, and other big acts and then took what they wanted from each and made a new blend. They carefully defined what they wanted, learned from people who had been successful, and then executed and implemented their own model. Define, learn, do.

9. Deliver what you yourself would love to have as a consumer.

Remember Paul's quote: "We wanted to be the band we'd never seen on stage. We kept going to a concert wanting to see what we were dreaming we would do." That's exactly right. With your business, profession, or job, deliver what you would like to receive.

10. Be willing to look foolish.

Be willing to get into some uncomfortable situations in order to make it. There may be times when you have to risk making a fool out of yourself in order to make something of yourself. If you're looking for a pleasing path, you'll probably never find a purposeful victory. It's people who aren't worried about the pleasing path but are all about the victory who generally make it big.

11. Be determined.

Rehearse endlessly, and perform every chance you get. Be about doing what it is you do. Do it consistently over time, and put in the hours to master your craft.

12. Serve your customers in every way you can.

You may need to be creative and serve them in a way no one has ever thought of before. Serendipitous benefits will come out of a true desire to serve your customer.

13. Once you have your formula right, stick to it.

KISS had all kinds of people trying to get them to change their formula, to mellow them out a little.

They could have backed off and gone along, been less extreme, eased up on the makeup or the stage craziness. They didn't. They knew they had it right and they stuck to it. Would they have made it if they hadn't seemed so crazy? It's doubtful.

14. Be humble, even when you make it.

The members of KISS never forgot their humble start. They worked hard and respected and interacted with their fans. They acted crazy on stage, but as people they always came across as genuine.

15. There's nothing wrong with becoming an original character.

Be bold, innovate with courage, and stand out from the crowd. Have the character to become an original character.

A LAPTOP AND
A DREAM

*The heart of entrepreneurship is never about
what we have. It's about what we do.*

—JESSICA JACKLEY

As a little girl, Jessica Jackley attended Sunday school every week in her small town of Franklin Park, Pennsylvania, learning stories from the Bible. One Sunday her teacher was talking about poverty and explained that people living in poverty didn't have the most basic needs we take for granted, like food, shelter, or clothing. Jesus loved the poor people, her teacher explained, and wanted everyone else to love them too. She told the class the story of the Good Samaritan and other stories.

As Jessica listened, she tried to follow along in her own illustrated children's Bible. She saw pictures of the poor: they were barefoot and filthy, they wore rags for clothing, some of them looked to be in great pain, and many of them were reaching up to beg for help. As she stared at the pictures, she heard her teacher quote, "What you do for the least of these you do for me." Something deep was stirred in Jessica's young heart.

She pondered that quote, asking questions like "Where are these poor people? What exactly should I do to help them?"

Then her teacher said something else that stunned her even more: "Jesus promised that the poor will always be with us." Jessica felt confused, then angry, and then scared as this sank in. She thought, *Why would God do this? What does this mean for me? Will my efforts all be wasted? Am I being set up to fail?* As she grew up, she heard more and more stories that convinced her that poverty was an enormous problem which could never be completely solved. People assured her that, while it was nice to try, no one could ever fix things or make a permanent difference. The images from her Bible began to be replaced by real-life images she saw in mailings and TV ads from charity organizations: starving people pleading for help, children with swollen bellies, babies who looked like skeletons. Everything felt removed from her suburban "Norman Rockwell" lifestyle.

When everyone she knew was healthy and well-fed, it was nearly impossible for her to wrap her brain around the dismal statistics, for instance, that half the world was living on less than two dollars a day, and 22,000 children died each day from poverty. But the marketing campaigns from nonprofits had their intended effect on her, and she started donating as much and as often as she could. She scoured her house for lost coins. She gave her weekly allowance to her congregation's tithing fund. She set up a Kool-Aid stand, sold magazine subscriptions, cookies, and chocolate bars door-to-door, and donated all her profits to charity. On Halloween she would take a UNICEF box and ask for donations while trick-or-treating.

She felt good doing all these things, but she knew something was missing: real contact with the people she felt called to help. Everything felt impersonal. It also felt like a bottomless hole—that no matter how much she or anyone else gave, there would never be enough donations to make any kind of substantial difference for these suffering people.

By the time she reached high school, she felt disillusioned and somewhat hardened by the donation process. But she was "still in love with the idea of saving the world,"[19] so she kept trying, this time as a more active participant instead of a donor on the sidelines. She jumped at every opportunity she could find to volunteer. Her experiences with volunteering also left her feeling deeply dissatisfied: nothing she did felt important or worthwhile. She was also frustrated by seeing the same people over and over again and wondered why the cycle of hunger and poverty couldn't be broken.

When she was a senior, an opportunity arose to serve in an orphanage in Haiti for spring break. She talked it over with her parents; they approved, and her dad even decided to go with her. She packed toys, soap, socks, and toothbrushes for the orphanage and set off. Her childhood dream was realized: she was personally interacting with impoverished orphans. Experiencing the contrast of how these children lived compared to her life changed her forever. But she still had an abiding doubt that the problem of poverty could ever be solved.

She was determined to make a valiant effort, however. So she went to college and studied philosophy, political science, and poetry at a liberal arts college. Her purpose, in her words, was to "learn how to ask the right questions, understand power, and harness language, respectively — all as part of an attempt to understand poverty and to equip myself to fight against it."[20] She graduated feeling "book-smart" but not "street-smart" about poverty and still didn't have a clue about how to effectively work on the problem. Without a plan, and having fallen in love with a boy who lived in California while at a conference in Washington DC, she headed west for an adventure.

She crammed in with a dozen recent graduates in a tiny apartment in Silicon Valley near her boyfriend Matt's house and close to Stanford University. The day after she landed, she took a pile of résumés and wandered around the Stanford campus, giving a résumé to anyone who would take one. She was hired as a temporary administrative assistant by Julie Juergens at the business school's Center for Social Innovation.

Although grateful for the job, she felt disappointed that she had landed at the business school. She believed that "people interested in business were by definition uninterested in solving important social problems."[21] The most successful business people could do, she thought, would be to make a bunch of money and then give it away someday. She worried that she was "selling out." To keep her eye on the prize, she took a second job in the evening and on weekends at a nonprofit halfway house for teen moms and their children, serving as a live-in "house mom" and on-site manager.

Despite her preconceptions, she quickly realized that there could not have been a better place for her to learn about social impact than the business school. Although not a student, she was able to attend lectures and conferences and visit with professors and students. She read case studies that were used as teaching materials in MBA classes. She learned about organizations that were changing the world in major ways.

Her views slowly began to shift, especially as she saw the contrast between the big, scalable social-change ventures she was studying and the small, local halfway house, where there was no vision for expansion and funding was always a problem. The organizations she studied at Stanford measured everything, while the kinds of change occurring at the halfway house were difficult if not impossible to measure. The halfway house board had faith and optimism, but not the best business sense.

She eventually resigned from her position at the halfway house and she and Matt married. She began thinking more deeply about what she wanted to do. Her sense was to combine the two worlds she had experienced—the business-smart, scalable organization on the one hand and the heart-driven, local charity on the other.

She said, "I envisioned an organization that connected individuals to one another in a deeply personal way, and then equipped them to inspire others, serving multitudes more."[22]

After her honeymoon she returned to work at the business school. One evening she received an e-mail announcing a lecture by a man she had never heard of who was going to talk about a different sort of banking that served the poor. Intrigued, she attended the lecture. She sat in fascination as Dr. Muhammad Yunus explained the microfinance work he was pioneering with his Grameen Bank. (This was in the fall of 2003, and Yunus would be awarded the Nobel Peace Prize for his work three years later.) Yunus had started his operation by lending just $26 to a poor woman to buy materials to make bamboo furniture. He extended his operations and was pleased to find that every woman paid back the loan in full and was able to expand her business because of the loan. Today, Grameen Bank has over 7.5 million borrowers, and more than two-thirds of them have lifted themselves out of extreme poverty.

Jessica was inspired by two things: first, the accessibility of working directly with the poor, and second, seeing the poor as driven entrepreneurs instead of helpless victims. Her understanding of poverty was turned on its head. She wanted to be involved, and her wheels started turning.

She decided to do exactly what Yunus had done: connect directly with the people whom she wanted to serve and listen carefully to what they needed. But she wasn't quite sure how to go about it, so she started interviewing dozens of people who might be able to give her pointers. She met Brian Lehnen, the founder of Village Enterprise, a nonprofit that focused on microenterprise in East Africa. When she explained to him what she wanted to do, she was surprised that he really got it. He said, "I think you're right. You can't really know what the problem of poverty is all about until you go and see it for yourself. You can't know until you are there, really spending time with entrepreneurs. Sounds like it's time for you to get out there."

The two continued to meet several more times over the next few weeks and ended up crafting a plan to send Jessica to East Africa to interview the entrepreneurs Village Enterprise served. She would spend three and a half months interviewing these entrepreneurs and finding out how the grant money had affected their lives. A few weeks later, she boarded a plane for Nairobi.

After dozens of interviews with enterprising women, one thing became abundantly clear to her: these women had much different priorities than what she would have imagined for them. "If I had been given some sort of magic wand," she said, "I would have confidently wielded it, believing I knew how to fix things and improve the lives of the people I so badly wanted to serve. But it didn't take me long to realize that I would have gotten a lot wrong."[23] She learned that the more she valued what mattered to the people she served—instead of imposing her perceptions and priorities onto them—the more useful she could be to them.

Her trip proved to be invaluable. She gained clarity about what could work and what wouldn't. She saw that combining a little bit of business training with a small infusion of capital could be life-changing for people. She saw how, by changing one person's life, the effects could be extended to his or her family and community as well. She was also surprised to learn how widespread Internet connectivity was throughout Africa, even in the poorest locations—an asset that could be leveraged.

Most important, she learned that these working poor were not defined by their poverty. Instead, they were smart, hardworking entrepreneurs. It wasn't all suffering and despair—there was tangible hope for them to climb out of poverty with just a little help. Not a single entrepreneur she interviewed asked for a handout or donation. They wanted loans so they could maintain ownership and autonomy. They wanted to help themselves, to feel independent and strong. And she could see how, in the vast majority of cases, a loan would be put to good use and would see a quick return.

By the time she returned home she had a clear vision of what she wanted to do: connect other people across the world with these entrepreneurs and their stories. She wanted to enable microlending all across the world, facilitated by volunteer crowd-sourced funds provided over the Internet. They drafted a mission statement: "To connect people through lending to alleviate poverty."

It was virgin territory—no one had ever conceived of doing something like this. She and Matt took their idea to one lawyer after another, only to be shut down each time. They all told them that what they wanted to do was illegal and impossible. It was far too risky, and there were far too many barriers.

Several months and more than forty lawyers later, they finally found one who volunteered to help: Kiran Jain. She believed in the potential of their idea more than she feared the risks. She helped them establish their nonprofit organization, Kiva. Jessica reported that all those meetings with lawyers taught them a lot but not what they had expected. She said, "We learned that while it is necessary at times to get experts' opinions, at the end of the day we were the only ones who could make the final call on whether or not to move forward."[24] The lawyers' job was to identify risk. Her and Matt's job, as entrepreneurs,

> "WHILE IT IS NECESSARY AT TIMES TO GET EXPERTS' OPINIONS, AT THE END OF THE DAY WE WERE THE ONLY ONES WHO COULD MAKE THE FINAL CALL ON WHETHER OR NOT TO MOVE FORWARD."
> —JESSICA JACKLEY

was to weigh the risks and find a way through the barriers.

They sifted through the piles of negative feedback they'd received from lawyers and went to work. Since there was no precedent for person-to-person lending over the Internet, the answers were hard to find. They cold-called anyone they felt could offer insights: bankers, economists, tech gurus, and nonprofit leaders. They finally found a solution: all loans would have to be offered at zero percent interest. Through the process, they learned to tell their story clearly and in ways that would resonate specifically with whomever she was talking to. They made connections that would prove to be invaluable later on.

By the spring of 2005, after a year of cold-calling and research, they had to make the decision whether to proceed or scrap the idea. They chose to launch. Jessica worked two jobs to fund a flight to Africa to find their first entrepreneurs to feature as borrowers on Kiva. She identified seven, collected all the information they needed, and headed home. Once home, she drafted an e-mail to friends and family, telling them about the project and asking them to each lend $25 to help entrepreneurs on the other side of the world. She hit send and they held their breath.

They were shocked when all the money they needed flooded in virtually overnight. Their first loans were executed. One of their partners in Africa gave the money to the entrepreneurs and then sent Jessica and Matt frequent updates on their progress. All those initial loans were repaid within months.

At the same time as the loans were being repaid, Jessica started classes at the Stanford Graduate School of Business to get her MBA degree. She was convinced she needed formal business training to scale Kiva to be as big and impactful as she envisioned. But even after receiving her MBA, she found herself wishing she had more specific knowledge about microfinance, finance, management, and more. She learned that "No amount of education will necessarily make you feel that you are ready to start something new.... We can always tell ourselves we need just one more thing, one more experience, before we are ready to go. But more often than not, we are ready right now, just as we are."[25]

By October 2005 they removed the "beta" from their website, and Kiva was official. They found new borrowers and secured new loans. In mid-November several popular blogs featured them and the resulting traffic took care of their supply of loans in just a few hours. They scrambled to find more borrower entrepreneurs. The initial blogosphere buzz was soon followed by mainstream press coverage, including features by *The Wall Street Journal*, CNN, ABC, NPR, and the BBC. One year after their launch, PBS aired a fifteen-minute documentary about them, which drove so much online traffic that their website crashed for three days. Once it was back up, $250,000 was loaned in one week. Within the next month they hit their million-dollar target.

Jessica reflected on the "rough edges" of their journey and how everything had been patched together from whatever resources they could pull together. For their first round of loans, for example, they didn't even have a way to process payments online. They bartered an old guitar to get their logo design. Their initial site was built by borrowing a neighbor's Wi-Fi. Jessica counsels,

> In the beginning of any venture, there will be rough edges.... You probably won't have everything you think you need.... You just have to show up and begin, be willing to learn as you go, and take steps

forward with whatever resources you have (or don't have)....

> "JUST ABOUT ANYTHING YOU CAN DO TODAY IS BETTER THAN DOING NOTHING, AND YOU'LL BE ABLE TO DO EVEN MORE TOMORROW IF YOU BEGIN WITH SOMETHING TODAY."
> —JESSICA JACKLEY

Just about anything you can do today is better than doing nothing, and you'll be able to do even more tomorrow if you begin with something today. When it's messy and imperfect, embrace it. Roll up your sleeves, get your hands dirty, and start.[26]

About a year and a half after their initial launch, Jessica and Matt faced a monumental test. They received a call from the director of a very well-funded social responsibility initiative for a well-known tech company who told them, "What you're doing is fantastic, and we want to help. We have $10 million to put into your project." However, it came with a catch: They didn't want to divide the $10 million into $25, $50, or $100 gift certificates to be used to make small loans on the site. Instead, they wanted it distributed as quickly as possible throughout the world and then returned. In other words, there would be no connective experience between lender and borrower, which was the hallmark of their mission.

Jessica turned the money down and pointed him to other organizations she thought would be a better fit. He was flabbergasted, for obvious reasons: *Who turns down $10 million?* Only those with a clear mission and the conviction to stay true to that mission no matter what. As Jessica explains, "Saying no to opportunities that don't match your mission, no matter how tempting they are, is the same as saying a resounding yes to the goals you have already committed yourself to."[27]

By the summer of 2007, Kiva had cleared $10 million in loans. By any measure, it was a stellar success. However, Jessica was devastated when they discovered that one of their partners in Uganda was nothing but a façade organization, and the leaders were keeping the lent money themselves—nearly $125,000—instead of passing it on to entrepreneurs in the region. She felt stupid, embarrassed, and betrayed.

> "SAYING NO TO OPPORTUNITIES THAT DON'T MATCH YOUR MISSION, NO MATTER HOW TEMPTING THEY ARE, IS THE SAME AS SAYING A RESOUNDING YES TO THE GOALS YOU HAVE ALREADY COMMITTED YOURSELF TO."
> —JESSICA JACKLEY

After thinking it through, she swallowed her pride and contacted every lender who had been affected, told them what happened, and refunded the lenders' money. This was an exception to their policy of having lenders assume the risk of loans. Jessica expected angry responses but was pleasantly surprised that the reaction from most lenders was overwhelmingly positive. People were grateful for their honesty and were even more trusting of Kiva. In fact, most of the lenders re-lent the money that had been refunded to them.

Jessica took the opportunity to tighten up their processes and reduce the chance of fraud. She says, "Only by being honest about what is working and what isn't working can organizations find ways to improve, together. Transparency draws people in. It shows them that they are not on the outside, but on the inside, experiencing the journey with you. No one expects perfect, but everyone does (and should) demand honesty and will be inspired by resilience."[28]

Kiva not only survived this crisis and many others, but today is thriving. Since 2005, Kiva has crowd-funded more than a million loans, totaling more than half a billion dollars, at a repayment rate of 99 percent. As of November 2013, Kiva was raising about $1 million every three days. The Kiva platform has attracted a community of more than a million lenders from around the world. And it was all started by one person with little but a laptop and a dream who learned "that real, positive change is possible. Poverty does not have to win in the end. And anyone who *wants* to participate in making the world better *can*. Even the most 'unqualified' individuals can contribute to great things; even the most humble efforts can end up improving the lives of thousands or millions of people."[29]

MINDSET MEMOS

1. You don't need anyone's approval or permission to make a difference.

At every turn, when everyone told Jessica "You can't do that," she pushed forward. She asked for advice but not permission. She saw a vision of what could be, took initiative, and just got it done.

Trailblazing can be scary, and to calm our fears, we often listen to everyone and everything else except the one thing that matters most: our own heart.

2. Start where you are, with what you have.

When Jessica started Kiva, she had no money, no advanced degree, very little experience, and very few connections. She could have easily focused on what she didn't have and let that stop her. But she didn't. She leveraged every resource she had to the fullest, and scraped together everything she didn't have. She didn't wait for the stars to align.

There's never a better time to start a venture than right now. You have everything you need to start, and everything you need to finish will appear as you persevere.

3. Identify and question prevailing assumptions.

Jessica entered the nonprofit world with assumptions about poverty and the people held in its grasp: they were powerless victims, donations were the only way to help, and there was no way to break the cycle for good.

But Jessica realized that all these assumptions were wrong. Some poor were enterprising, driven, innovative, hardworking entrepreneurs who just needed a toehold. A relatively tiny amount of money could make a huge and lasting difference.

In whatever you're trying to achieve, no matter the field or industry, there are popular assumptions about what is true, what works and what doesn't work, what is possible. Leaders question assumptions and break through the boundaries of the known to create new, world-changing possibilities.

4. Question your own assumptions.

Jessica arrived at Stanford with a worldview about business and entrepreneurs: that business existed solely for profit and couldn't be leveraged to enact social change, and that entrepreneurs only cared about money. She discovered instead that entrepreneurship is one of the most powerful social forces on the planet and that entrepreneurs are leading the charge for social change.

What unidentified and unquestioned assumptions do you carry that prevent you from seeing things clearly and hinder your progress?

5. Don't unquestioningly accept the advice of experts; they are often just protecting their own turf and speaking from their own biases.
Jessica went through more than forty lawyers who all told her Kiva was a foolish and impossibly risky idea before she found one who would help. While all the "experts" were telling her every reason it couldn't be done, she fought her way through loopholes and around barriers to find a way to make it work.

Experts can certainly be valuable resources to learn from. But understand that their knowledge is not perfect, and they are subject to their own biases. Don't ignore their advice out of naiveté or stubbornness, but also don't accept their advice as the gospel truth. For every great human accomplishment there were scores of experts lined up lecturing that it wouldn't work.

6. Get in the trenches.

From a young age Jessica had ideas of what she wanted to do. But she couldn't implement them effectively until she climbed down into the trenches and worked with people one-on-one to discover what they valued and how to work with them.

Ideas are valuable and can certainly get you started. But ultimately, you have to get your hands dirty to find out what really works. You have to test and measure, refine and test again.

7. Find out what's important to other people, and work on their level.

Until Jessica worked with people individually, she was prone to imposing her ideas of what they *should* value onto them, rather than understanding what *they* actually valued.

To motivate and inspire people as a leader, you have to know what they value. You have to work with them on their terms. As an entrepreneur, you have nothing of value to offer until you know what other people want and need.

8. Entrepreneurship and leadership are messy— learn to be okay with it.

Chaos is uncomfortable—so much so that most people can't stomach it. There's a reason why there are relatively few leaders and entrepreneurs.

If you want to accomplish anything great in life, you've got to learn to work with chaos and confusion. You won't always have everything you want, but you always have everything you need to take the next step, however messy.

9. Stay true to your mission and fight the temptation to drift off course.

It's so easy to lose sight of the core mission and vision—both because of difficulties as well as things that appear to be fortuitous windfalls. Leaders are clear on their values and goals and stick to them no matter what.

10. Be open and transparent about your mistakes. Take responsibility.

There's never really any other viable choice when you mess up. No one is perfect, and no one expects you to be perfect. We're drawn to people who are honest and who take responsibility, even if we've been adversely affected. Own up to your mistakes immediately and openly, and people will respect you for it.

It's Difficult to Play Simple

It's better to go down with your own vision than with someone else's.

—Johan Cruijff

In the summer of 2010 the World Cup was to be held in South Africa. Spain was the odds-on favorite to win, and they did, in fact, win the whole thing cleanly and without a lot of opposition. They were a joy to watch.

Spain had a way of playing that clearly displayed they were the best team in the world. In the World Cup, each country gathers its top players and makes a sort of all-star team out of them, and then the countries play each other. It's like the Olympics, except this is strictly for soccer. Spain had a certain style involving superior ball skills, one-touch passing, and a demoralizing way of dominating the possession of the ball. They would pass the ball around as in a game of keep-away and not let the other team touch it.

They were able to finish smoothly and seemingly without effort at the goal.

Commentators surmised they were not only the best country team in the world but maybe even the best World Cup team of all time. Their style was quickly becoming known as "Spanish fútbol." Other teams were seeking to emulate their success.

Spain beat the Netherlands in the finals, which was ironic, because "Spanish fútbol" didn't originate in Spain. It was actually Dutch, and that particular World Cup final was the classic case of the student outgrowing the teacher.

To understand this story, you have to go all the way back to the Spanish Civil War. In 1936, Generalissimo Francisco Franco took power and ruled the country as dictator until his death in 1975. You might be wondering what that has to do with Spain winning the World Cup in 2010.

During Franco's long reign, he kept Spain more or less isolated from the rest of Europe, and it was difficult for international soccer players to play in Spain. It was also difficult for Spanish players to play in other countries. That is not the norm for Europe. The players in Europe have historically migrated all over different countries. They've played in each other's leagues so much, they've had to make rules restricting a team to a certain number of foreign players.

Because Spain was so isolated, the quality of its soccer suffered. Meanwhile, the game in the rest of Europe had flourished, coming into its own as a modern professional sport and entertainment. Spain was largely left behind.

Authors Simon Kuper and Stephan Szymanski wrote that what saved Spain's soccer was the country's opening to Europe and the world at the end of Franco's rule. Spanish isolation began to break down in the last years of Franco's life. In 1973, just after Spain reopened its borders to foreign soccer players, Football Club of Barcelona imported the great Dutchman Johan Cruijff. It is possible to draw a direct line between Cruijff's arrival in Barcelona and Spain's victory in Johannesburg thirty-seven years later.[31]

The story gets going with one of the strangest financial arrangements in sports history. Because Franco's regime blocked the payment by Spanish companies to foreigners for anything, in order to acquire the player Johan Cruijff, FC Barcelona had to classify him as a piece of agricultural equipment. But Cruijff was no tractor. He was possibly the sport of soccer's premier leader.

Every true leader has what Noel Tichy calls a "teachable point of view." Other authors have called it a managerial philosophy. Every great leader, whatever his field of operations, has some sort of main idea — some theme he is promoting. It is his secret to success, his formula.

In Cruijff's case, it was one word: *pass*, as in "pass the ball." That was Cruijff's expertise. Of course, it was more complicated than just how one kicks a ball to someone else. It involved exactly how all the players on the pitch were to behave during passing. Player number one would have the ball, about to pass it to player number two. Player number three, within that same zone, was supposed to be in motion anticipating the pass from number two.

The players would anticipate the pass before player one ever passed the ball to player two. They would work in triangles for what are called "give-and-goes": one player passes to another and then takes off running, while the player receiving passes the ball to where the first player is going to be.

Cruijff talked about passing all the time. He never declined, rejected, or turned down a chance to talk about the importance of passing and could talk about it for hours on end. Passing was his teachable point of view, and he not only taught it, he preached it.

He played at Barcelona for most of the 1970s. The coach was also Dutch. Together they brought a version of what was called the "Dutch touch" to Spanish fútbol. Spain had never seen anything like it.

Cruijff had planned to retire after he finished playing for Barcelona, but he lost all his money in bad investments. That may have been a terrible thing for Cruijff to go through personally, but it turned out to be very fortuitous for the future of Spanish soccer. The irony was that the guy who had been brought in and paid for as a piece of agricultural equipment had lost most of his money investing in a pig farm.

Cruijff needed to make more money, so instead of retiring, he had to go play in the tiny North American league, and then he finished his career back in the Netherlands playing for his home club, Ajax. He was able to play his final few years in the town in which he had grown up and then retired in 1984.

A year later, he was named Ajax's manager. He had started to play in the club's league for kids when he was just three years old, and now he was leading the team. Upon being named manager, he said three words, "Everything must change." He had plans. He once said, "Everything I did before I was thirty years old I did on instinct. After I was thirty I began to understand why."[32]

> "EVERYTHING I DID BEFORE I WAS THIRTY YEARS OLD I DID ON INSTINCT. AFTER I WAS THIRTY I BEGAN TO UNDERSTAND WHY."
> —JOHAN CRUIJFF

He had gained great experience and was just a naturally great player. As he grew older, he could analyze what he was doing, understand why it was working, and turn that into a teachable philosophy. He could understand the science of the game.

One of the most important moves he made was to spend time working with the club's youth teams. In the United States we just call our sports franchises teams. The Pittsburgh Steelers, for instance, are a professional football team. The concept of a "club" is quite a bit different. Not all the participants in a club are professionals. There is a professional team at the top, but the club has teams beginning with small children, all the way up to academy teams, reserve teams, practice teams, etc. That way, the clubs can instill their philosophy into players from their earliest years, creating a pipeline of talent from which the pro and semipro teams draw.

Cruijff went to the kids' teams of various ages to check on the development of players for the club. He had a different way of looking at this process. He said, "We're no longer going to focus on winning matches for these kids. Instead, we'll focus entirely on developing talented boys into adult stars."

He wasn't saying they weren't going to keep score and not care at all about winning. He wasn't thinking the kids were overcompetitive and might get their feelings hurt. That was the farthest thing from his mind. He didn't want them trying to win a short-term match at the expense of becoming better players long-term. There are times in life when you miss out on making the mistake that could have taught you the very thing you needed in order to be more successful in your future. We can sacrifice long-term growth by being too caught up in the current little battles we are fighting.

Cruijff wanted to make sure his youth teams weren't making this mistake. He told the coaches they would no longer be evaluated on whether they won or lost but on how well their charges learned and applied the funda-mental principles he was trying to instill. Even the worst team can win once in a while. Winning is the goal, but development is how that goal is met. Sacrificing develop-ment in order to win will result in fewer wins long-term.

Cruijff stressed the fundamentals of passing, position, and possession. He stressed the development of the players in these areas. He valued "two-footed" players—those who could kick as well with one foot as they could with the other.

He taught the importance of position. "One of the biggest parts about winning a game is just being in the right spot," he said. Steve Sabol of NFL Films, one of the people who was influential in building that league up into the icon it is today, said, "Good players are either in the right place or they're there at the right time. Great players do both." Cruijff made sure his players knew where to be on the field, and when.

Passing was his biggest point of emphasis. He developed drills that sharpened the passing fundamentals, and he ran them incessantly. His drills would train boys to do the right things by instinct—making triangles, getting numerical advantage, speed of action, one-touch passing, receiving the ball, small spaces, pressuring opponents. All of these teachable point-of-view elements were taught by way of his drills.

Cruijff would often pit his boys against older teams in which they would have to make up for their smaller size with better tactics. He would deliberately play his boys out of position to see if they could adjust to being in the wrong spot. He would mix them up so every player knew the other players' positions, to some extent. Then, when they were playing against other teams, they would better understand the position against which they were defending.

Cruijff also looked for lessons from other disciplines. He brought in opera singers to teach the boys how to properly breathe. He brought in a Ping-Pong champion to teach them how to deal with stress. He brought in a gardener to teach them how to take care of their gear.

Kuper and Szymanski wrote, "At one time they brought in a promising youngster who had never made it to have him explain where he had gone wrong." Imagine being fifteen, and your coaches bring in an eighteen-year-old whose own promise has petered out. He tells you exactly why he didn't make it. It will get your attention.

He taught all the teams, from the youngest to the top professionals, in one uniform way. Everybody played the same formation. Everybody played with the same philosophy, style, and fundamentals. Everyone knew automatically what to do in every situation, and the younger talent could easily move up and understand what was going on when they reached the higher-level teams.

Cruijff left Ajax in 1988, but the club has always followed his model. He returned to it as an older man in 2011 as a sort of figurehead. Over the past twenty-plus years a steady stream of top-level talent has poured out of Ajax, exactly as Cruijff designed it to happen. He not only set up a way where he personally could make great leaders; he made it a point to develop players who would turn into great player-leaders. This machinery he put in place continued to work for two decades after he had left.

The accomplishment is impressive. Cruijff's leadership legacy is that he instilled a philosophy into an organization, and it lasted. It worked with and without him as the leader. That's a rare leadership feat.

Many clubs all around the world have youth teams and an intentional development program, but for the most part they don't get anywhere near Ajax's results. The head of Ajax's youth academy said, "It's not a recipe for pancakes," meaning this isn't an easy thing to copy. It is a recipe, but it's not a simple one. Few have come even close to replicating it.

One club that has begun to get the same caliber of results, year in and year out, has followed the Cruijff recipe exactly. The reason they have it is because when Cruijff left Ajax in 1988, he was hired to be Barcelona's head coach. Impressed with what Cruijff had done in Holland, and having had a relationship with him as a player, Spain brought him back.

The first day on the job, where did he go? To see the youth play, of course. The very first day he spotted a kid named Pep Guardiola, a teenager. "Who's that skinny kid out there in the middle? Move him up to the first team." He hadn't even seen the first team yet. Pep Guardiola played at that top level for Barcelona for over ten years. He later became their head coach and continued Cruijff's teachable point of view. He has managed teams to victory in the Spanish, German, European, and world championships since then. He's one of the most dominant soccer managers and was a big star player. Cruijff picked him out in five minutes of watching him on a field.

Barcelona was given a transfusion of Cruijff-ism. Today, Barcelona's La Masia Farmhouse Youth Academy is the envy of the world. They take a long-term view of player development and systematically churn out a steady stream of top players. They don't worry about competition all that much, matches are treated like classes, and they don't care about a player's size. Soccer is one of the few sports in which you don't have to be a freak of nature with certain physical proportions. One of the best players in the world today plays for Barcelona at 5'6" in height. As a matter of fact, the average height on FC Barcelona today is 5'7.75".

They don't test for physical capacity at La Masia. They don't even care how fast players are. Players hardly ever do fitness training unless they have the ball at their feet. In their way of thinking, one can't get fit without the ball. Everything is done with a ball at one's feet. They only train for about ninety minutes a day. Some of the academies around the world are like boot camps. They drill all day long. Not Barcelona. They figure that if you teach kids right, ninety minutes per day is plenty.

When asked why they train so little, they responded, "Well, does it look like we need to do more?" They further commented, "Besides that, these are schoolboys. They need to be schooled. They need to have an education, because most of them aren't going to make it in soccer and they're our family, and we don't want to just grind them up and spit them out on the street with nothing else to do in their life and only take the one percent who are actually going to make it."

When Spain emerged from its isolation, it became a soccer powerhouse, largely through FC Barcelona. When Spain won that World Cup, seven of the players on the victorious Spanish national team were from the Cruijff system. Interestingly, seven players on the defeated Holland side came through the Ajax system. Fourteen of the players playing at the highest level of soccer in the world had been trained through Cruijff's philosophy. "It's wonderfully appropriate," wrote Kuper and Szymanski, "that the Spaniards sealed their rise in a World Cup final against their mentor country. This was the Cruijff versus Cruijff final. Probably for the first time, both teams in soccer's biggest game were, in their origins, the product of one man." Author David Winter added, "Holland's path to the world title is blocked by the more authentic version of their better selves. It is now Spain who played Dutch soccer the best."

MINDSET MEMOS

1. Isolation stifles growth and innovation.

When the Iron Curtain was lifted and the Eastern Bloc countries were suddenly free to commingle with the West, the people quickly reconnected and bonded together because of shared national heritage and ethnic and cultural ties. In matters of technology, however, the divide was quite a shock. On the Western side you had someone driving a brand new Mercedes S-Class, and on the Eastern side you had someone driving a Trabant with a smoking tailpipe and a two-stroke engine. Both cars were built in Germany at the same time.

To innovate, create, and grow in knowledge and ability, you have to circulate. You have to associate with others with similar goals. Ideas grow when they are shared.

2. To attract top talent, you have to be creative.

In order to play in Spain, Cruijff had to be classified as agricultural equipment. You sometimes have to work around the red tape if you want to get the best of the best to work with you. Ben Horowitz, former CEO of Opsware and LoudCloud, said, "You cannot build a world-class team or company without world-class people." That seems obvious, but most people and businesses don't operate with that principle. It may take creativity and some work to put the right team together. It might not be straightforward, but it will be worth the extra effort.

3. Intentionally develop a pipeline of talent.

Always be thinking about your pipeline and developing who's next. When you have children, you are always thinking what each child needs, and as they grow older, you want to make sure their developmental needs are met. In a business, you should have people you are working with who might not be ready for heavy responsibilities just yet, but you are working with them and thinking about what they need in order to grow and develop. Build your teams the way you build your family.

4. A real leader has a brand, a philosophy, and a teachable point of view.

Could someone look at your work or your business and identify what your teachable point of view is? Would someone be able to sermonize about your philosophy by observing your actions? If not, then maybe you don't have one, or maybe you haven't communicated it enough.

How about in your family? Do your kids know what you stand for? Do they know your top three principles?

5. The great ones in anything are incredibly active.
Does it sound as if Cruijff took the leadership positions he did because of the money and perks? Does it sound as if he did what he did so that he could drive a fancy car? He worked nonstop. He took extra time, apart from being the head of the pro team, to work with youth. He was into what he was doing and did more than the job required.

The best leaders are overly active and involved. They think about their work or business all the time. Their brain won't stop working on it. They diligently work to make it the best it can be.

6. Sometimes apparent setbacks lead to tremendous blessings.
How would Cruijff's story possibly have played out if he hadn't lost all his money on the bad pig farm investment? If he had made a whole bunch of money instead and been set for life, would he have become a manager? Maybe, maybe not. His loss ensured that he got there, though. He turned his loss into a great legacy of leadership.

7. Learn the "why" behind your instincts.

There is something called unconscious competence. A person might be good at something and not even realize it, and he can't tell you what he does that makes him good. Analyze it and figure out why you are good at what you're just naturally good at. Cruijff did that in his transition from player to coach. When he was able to understand that his game wasn't about talent or being the most athletic guy on the field, he saw that it was the ability to pass and to be in the right place at the right time. He was then able to figure out how to teach it and how to identify it in the players he was coaching.

As a side point, if you are too busy to think, you are too busy to lead. Action should come only after thinking it through. A leader is the one who thinks it through, understands what needs to be done, and only then goes out and makes it happen.

8. Don't sacrifice long-term growth for short-term success.

This principle is counterintuitive, but if you are so afraid to fail that you stop growing, you have sacrificed the level of success that you can achieve.

9. Drill on the fundamentals consistently.

Find the essential core. There are a lot of good things you can do in any endeavor, but there are just a few essential and great ones. Simplify, and then work those few basic, essential fundamentals until you master them.

Cruijff said, "Soccer is simple, but it is difficult to play simple." He understood what he stood for and what he wanted and didn't let the complexities take over. Making something simple is some of the hardest work you'll do. But it pays.

10. Stay consistent with your philosophy.
In Cruijff's system, the little kids were taught the same philosophy as the older and professional teams. The pipeline was smooth and the transition seamless.

11. Observe other disciplines to learn first principles.
You can learn from anything, anywhere, at any time, from anyone. You can learn from automakers, space explorers, founding fathers, education innovators, sports figures, business figures, inventors, and artists. All the different walks of life have something to teach each other. Principles of success apply, no matter the discipline to which you apply them.

12. One person can make a difference.
Cruijff was the obvious magic-maker in two different organizations. His philosophy proved itself, and he was the guy with the formula and touch to make it work.

CHAPTER

5

ELECTRIC LEADERSHIP

*When something is important enough, you do
it even if the odds are not in your favor.*

—ELON MUSK

If you're familiar with Tesla electric cars, you know
how disruptive they've been to the auto industry. Behind
this car are a lot of powerful entrepreneurs and some great
minds and innovators, but chief among them is Elon Musk.

Elon Musk is an entrepreneur who earned both
his business and physics degrees at the University of
Pennsylvania. He almost began a PhD program in applied
physics at Stanford but quit so he could start a software
company. He built that company for a few years and sold
it to Compaq for more than $300 million while still in his
early twenties. Then he got involved with a little company
called PayPal. He was one of the geniuses behind PayPal,
who sold that to eBay after just three years for $1.5 billion.

Not bad earnings in your twenties for three years' worth of work.

Elon is driven by a vision that, long-term, humans need to be a "multi-planetary species." Talk about a big dream! He started digging into what NASA was doing. In his mind, Mars was the primary target for colonization and settlement, and he was disappointed that NASA had no real plans to even explore Mars, much less build a colony there.

Here you had a government that wasn't even thinking about exploring a planet that a private sector entrepreneur was interested in colonizing. Talk about a difference in mindset! But Musk didn't look at what NASA was doing and try to improve on it. Instead, he used his physics background to start a private company called SpaceX, which stands for Space Exploration Technologies Corporation. It became the first private company to deliver cargo to the space station. The company has picked up billions of dollars of orders from NASA and other countries to deliver supplies to the space station.

Such an endeavor is pretty impressive and intimidating for most of us. You're probably wondering, "How'd he come up with this? How did he pull it off?" First of all, Musk innovates by using what he calls *first principles thinking*. In an interview he explained, "I think it's important to reason from first principles rather than by analogy. The normal way we conduct our lives is we reason by analogy. [With analogy] we are doing this because it's like something else that was done, or it is like what other people are doing. [With first principles] you boil things down to the most fundamental truths…and then reason up from there."[33] This methodology enables innovation in big leaps rather than building small improvements onto things that already exist.

> THIS METHODOLOGY ENABLES INNOVATION IN BIG LEAPS RATHER THAN BUILDING SMALL IMPROVEMENTS ONTO THINGS THAT ALREADY EXIST.

Using his first principles thinking, he thought about it like this: To lift X pounds into orbit would take Y amount of fuel, which requires Z dollars in raw materials. So if you build a rocket to lift a certain amount of weight, you need to spend so many dollars in raw materials to make that happen.

According to *Wired* magazine, it turned out that Y plus Z was barely *two percent* of what NASA was spending per rocket launch. What was actually required to do it, according to his calculations, was two percent of what a government was spending to do the same thing. No wonder he was able to come in and get the contract! In every other hardware solution Musk was familiar with, total cost never dwarfed raw materials by anything close to 98 percent.[34]

Elon realized that something was way out of balance — and that government inefficiency and waste had become his opportunity. It's reminiscent of Fred Smith and what he did with Federal Express. The government seemed to have a lock on package delivery, and Smith came along and figured out a way to do it much better and created an entirely new industry. He has been so successful at it that the post office now feels the need to advertise in order to compete.

This idea that individual innovators can come in and do the job better and more efficiently also brings to mind the rush of education alternatives to state-sponsored schooling that are happening right now. Think of private schools and homeschooling. Another area is the rise of military contractors, using ex-soldiers who can guard ambassadors and dignitaries in dangerous places around the world much more efficiently than a bureaucratic government. The health care industry is another example of this idea. Private companies are setting up offshore medical facilities for those who can afford to get there, to dodge more force-based policies and ideas that are prevalent in countries where the government runs or is beginning to run the health care industry.

It makes you wonder, what else is the government doing that a private enterprise could do better? Anything, probably. Make a list of what the government is doing. It's a long list. As the government takes over more and more things, there is opportunity being created for entrepreneurs and innovators to step in and show that they can do it better while also saving tax money.

Elon didn't know the details that would be needed to forge a path to a privately held entrepreneurial space company. He didn't know how it would actually work. Hundreds of innovations were still required to take his idea to fruition, but the underlying physics gave him the confidence that he could pull it off. The numbers were sound.

His vision was ultimately that the human species needed to cultivate other planets on which to live, but at the same time he wanted to do more to preserve the one on which we are already living.

It's common to find people today who believe we're going to destroy our planet and that we're all doomed. There's a lot of pressure on government to "do something." When we get concerned that something is out of control, we look for a source of power to take action to fix what doesn't seem right. Sometimes people get really concerned about the problem — in this case the destruction of the planet.

Nobody should argue against keeping earth clean for future generations. However, people have widely different ideas on how to do it, and this often leads to anger and a maniacal obsession for some to have governments enforce their policies on people in a way that would encroach on basic rights and freedoms. The government-led, top-down approach almost never works. As we've seen with the space example, governmental "solutions" are usually the most expensive and inefficient.

Musk took a different approach. He analyzed an industry that many people think is wrecking the planet, the auto industry. And instead of using his money to pressure government to impose regulations on carmakers, pushing policies like carbon taxes, global cap and trade, corporate average fuel economies, emissions standards, and all kinds of regulations, he became an automaker himself.

His thinking seems to have been that he could better solve the problems with innovation rather than force — that the private sector, the entrepreneurs and innovators could accomplish something the public sector perhaps could not. He became the lead investor and controlling interest in Tesla Motors, the first successful all-new US car company in more than fifty years. It's amazing that it could even happen.

To top it off, instead of building their cars overseas where labor is cheap, they build them in California. Musk's vision was to make electric cars that not only weren't legislated to be built but people would actually love to own. Instead of working on the force model, he created a product that would be so attractive that people would *want* to buy it. He went for the entrepreneurial model.

To accomplish this, Musk had to go back to his first principles. Electric cars, as a concept, are not new. Concepts and prototypes date as far back as the early 1900s. However, there were insurmountable challenges with making them practical or desirable. First of all, they had limited range. The next problem was the batteries. Car batteries are quite heavy, which makes it very difficult to get decent range. The weight also makes it difficult to change the batteries in an electric car or to swap out in a hurry instead of having to charge them. Another significant challenge is that battery technology is quite expensive. Finally, what do you do with the battery at the end of its life? That material never goes away, so it's not entirely clean.

Definite and difficult issues have kept electric cars from becoming practical. This combination of obstacles made electric cars unappealing to automakers and consumers alike. Of course, there are others making electric cars. There's a new one from Japan called the Leaf, for instance, and it's a decent little people's car. The failed Fisker car from Europe was another example. But none of the electric cars on the market have come even close to what Musk and his colleagues have accomplished at Tesla.

The key breakthrough for Tesla was to use lithium ion battery technology. These have been proven for powering phones and laptops. But no one had thought of using them in cars before, and for good reason — lithium ion batteries are expensive. Their advantage is that they have a much higher energy density than any other kind of battery — you can get more energy stored into a light little lithium ion battery than you can in any other type. Also, the prevalence of this type of battery in our personal devices has resulted in the price going down significantly as the technology has improved.

If you could combine enough lithium ion cells into a single battery, you could not only get the range you needed, but you could also get sports car level performance. And if it could be done at an affordable price, the potential market would be huge.

With all successful leadership, there is a pattern. It starts with a vision. Notice that Musk didn't get involved with Tesla merely so he could be rich. He invested lots of money in the idea. You don't start a car company in the United States — or anywhere, for that matter — very cheaply these days. This wasn't a get-rich-quick scheme for him. He had a vision for something he (and Tesla's original founders) wanted to accomplish, and he believed, based on physics and fundamentals, that it could be done. A lot of innovation had to occur before it would actually happen, but he knew that, scientifically, it could be done and that it should be done. It got to the point for him where it *had* to be done. That's true vision.

> WITH ALL SUCCESSFUL LEADERSHIP, THERE IS A PATTERN. IT STARTS WITH A VISION.

Next, ideas and innovations are needed to make the vision possible. Between what's imagined and what can be done there's a road to follow. Nobody knows the path yet, so the best leaders actually *lead* people, creating systems and technology to get to places where no one has been before. That is what Musk did. He realized there had to be ideas and innovations to make the vision possible.

Then, once you have the vision and the innovation to bring it to reality, you develop a strategic game plan to bring these innovations to fruition. Finally, you must execute. Without any one of these factors — a vision, ideas and innovations to make the vision a reality, a game plan for implementation, and execution with excellence — you're not going to make it.

Musk and his colleagues had the vision, the ideas, the innovation, and now they needed a game plan that was just as powerful. His game plan was brilliant: Start with a very appealing and very expensive roadster. When you're selling to that market your customer has purely discretionary money. This meant they could charge a high price and get the company some traction.

Once the expensive roadster became successful, they reasoned, they could fund the continued development of the next car down the pecking order, which would be a sleek and sexy sports sedan, which would appeal to a much broader audience than the roadster. The success of that sedan would bring in enough revenue to continue to fund the company to where they could eventually come out with a relatively affordable entry-level people's car that almost anyone could buy.

Of course, everybody in the auto industry thought it was hilarious that some tech gurus from Silicon Valley believed they could enter a 120-year-old industry and teach the established companies how to do it. There was no shortage of critics in the auto industry who said it couldn't and wouldn't be done. Lots of people have tried, they said; lots of great cars have been prototyped and never seen the light of day. But Musk and his team pushed on anyway.

The plan began to work. Tesla's sporty Model S gained traction. It wasn't easy, of course. In the terrible financial year of 2008, Musk was forced to throw in the last of his personal funds to keep the development of the Model S alive. As we came out of the 2008 downturn and the slow, slow recovery of the economy, certain people with discretionary funds, who were concerned about the planet, were interested in a performance car that was also electric and good for the environment. The Model S began to sell.

Those sales have funded Tesla's growth. In the first three quarters of 2013, revenue at Tesla was up more than twelvefold! By the end of the year the company had brought in over $2 billion. The most registered vehicle in eight of the twenty-five most expensive zip codes in the US is a Tesla Model S. Sales of the Model S have continued to grow until the time of this writing, and the car has won numerous awards for quality and performance.

The car has elegant lines and lots of innovations besides its electric motor. It's got door handles that pop out when you get near the car. As soon as you get in the car, they suck back in. As soon as you put your seatbelt on, the car is on. You don't start an electric car—it's already on and ready to go. Another great feature is in the backseat. You open up a hatch, and you can have two car seats for kids installed backwards. The car has seemingly countless cool features, it's slick, and it performs incredibly well.

The base model goes from zero to 60 in 5.4 seconds. Top speed is 125 miles an hour, and it can travel as far as 250 miles. The tailpipe emissions, as they like to advertise, are zero. In fact, it doesn't even have tailpipes. The souped-up P90D version goes 0 to 60 in 2.8 seconds. Top speed for the P90D is 155 miles an hour, and it has 762 horsepower.

It's astounding what they've done with an electric car. You can get one for as low as $70,000, and you can get a $7,500 federal government tax credit (and even more in some states) for buying an electric vehicle.

What can we learn from this interesting story of a great visionary? There are all kinds of lessons to learn from Elon Musk's story, and he's really only just begun. Musk will go down in history as one of the world's all-time great innovators.

Here are some of the top lessons to be learned:

MINDSET MEMOS

1. A formal education can be useful.
Musk obtained degrees both in physics and in business. Interestingly, that's the combination that he's used to succeed in every one of these cases, but it's also not the degree or credential itself that has mattered for him. Notice he didn't use his degrees as credibility. At no point did he use his degree to get a good job; rather he used it to start companies. In fact, he has started four companies in succession that have all worked. A real education, not just pieces of paper to hang on a wall, is what has mattered for Musk.

2. Innovation is driven by a vision for something bigger and better.
This works in big ways and small. It doesn't really matter what you're working on. You could have a vision for how your family should operate harmoniously compared to how it operates now, and you can look at that gap between where you are and where

you'd like to be and innovate on ways to improve from your current position to your goal.

This principle of vision applies to anything—any area of personal improvement, any area of technological improvement. The tension of a vision for something better pulls you upward in that direction, and it can't be accomplished without something new: new behaviors, new technology, new steps, new relationships, new contributions, new understanding, and new knowledge. A hunger for something better is important because what a tragic life it would be not to have a vision for betterment in multiple categories of your life. What a tragedy just to burn up each day, eat some food, drink some water, suck down some oxygen, sleep it off a little bit, start up the next day and accomplish nothing—not trying to get better, not looking forward toward and being inspired by a vision.

The time that you'll feel most alive and have the most fun is when you're after a vision—when you have a positive tension on you for what could be versus what already is. The healthiest, most productive people are those who are in the mode of that positive tension to improve something, whether it's themselves, their relationships and their professional life, their business, their job, their corporation, or whatever it is. Create a tension-causing vision for what could be, compared to what actually is.

3. Don't be surprised when experts and critics are wrong.

Several times when it came to Elon Musk, critics and experts were just dead wrong. All the experts on space exploration and rocket science said Musk could never do what he has done. Now he has proven the use of reusable rockets for more efficient space travel. Musk consistently confounds the critics and innovates right past the so-called experts.

4. Conviction—not certainty—drives success.

Musk said he wasn't sure they would be able to solve the challenges of batteries in automotive application. But he had the math, and the math seemed to work. He actually thought that in one or two of these ventures he'd probably fall on his face, but the chances seemed too good not to try. He wasn't certain, but he was convinced.

There's a difference between conviction and certainty. You can be convinced and head off on a journey without knowing for sure that all the lights between you and your destination are green. You can be convinced that in some way or another you'll find a way to get through any red lights along the way. That's how leaders do it. Many times a leader charges up a hill yelling "Follow me!" and then turns back around thinking, "Oh my goodness, they're following me. I don't know if this is going to work. I've not been here myself either. I'm just convinced that this could work, that this should work, that this has to work, and I'm the one driving it, and others are believing it."

Leadership isn't plowing a field and going back and getting people and helping them plow the field you just plowed. Leadership is plowing new ground and being so convinced that it could and should be done that others join up with you. Conviction and absolute certainty are two very different things. You don't have to have total certainty, you just have to be convinced about your vision and work hard enough to figure out there's probably a way, and you can find it.

5. Don't let initial success define or distract you.
Some people never get beyond their first success, when actually what they're supposed to do is build one success on top of another. Steve Jobs did it — he pioneered the personal computer for the mass market, and then he revolutionized the music industry followed by the animated movie industry and the telecommunication industry. Four industries in twenty years for one guy. What would have happened if he had been so pleased with his wealth as a young man with personal computers that he

stopped and rested on his laurels? He'd be a mere footnote in history.

Like Jobs, Musk's goal wasn't success itself or to make a bunch of money and cash out. Even after his initial successes with his first software company and then with PayPal, he had a vision for something even bigger. Each success has been but a steppingstone for the next.

You can follow this pattern as well, even if on a smaller scale. You don't have to invent four industries or find yourself making rockets to go into outer space, but you can build on your successes in life and develop a momentum. If the goal is success, you'll cherish it like an idol. But if you use success as a tool toward greater contribution, it becomes the fuel and the fire for your next victory. This is the difference between one-hit wonders and continual successes, people who really and truly contribute in big ways in the world.

6. Move in where others are inefficient or haven't innovated enough.

Musk's opportunity was the lack of excellence in the work of others, whether it was in the government or the established auto companies. Out of all the hundreds of car companies that have been in business on this planet in the last century, you'd think that someone would have come up with the idea of using different types of batteries to power electric cars. It seems crazy, but that lack of innovation became a huge opportunity.

7. Invest in yourself.

Musk was willing to invest again and again in himself and his conviction to his vision. We have been sold on the idea that investing is skimming off a little bit of your money and handing it to a professional, and then waiting until you're done working a job you hate. That is not the right notion of investing. Investing should be that you take all the fruits of your labor, and the gifts and talents that you have been given, and then invest them back into what you do. You pour them back into what you are in control of, to reignite your own fires.

I know people who are in business for themselves, and a big percent of their precious cash flow they are willing to give to a financial professional to invest in stocks—other people's businesses. Meanwhile, their own business is starving for want of capital. Feed your own golden goose first because you control it.

Musk has always invested in what he had his hands on himself. The best money you'll ever invest is into your own vision.

8. Innovate through unlikely combinations.

The best, most cataclysmic type of innovation is when you take two different things and combine them in a way no one yet has done. You see this very clearly with Elon Musk, especially in his later companies. The power of combining two categories, in his case physics and private enterprise, has proven immensely successful for him. Steve Jobs did it by living at the intersection of telecommunications technology and liberal arts. What is *your* combination?

9. Don't buy into the apparent limitations of what's been done before.

Don't be held back by a frontier others have reached or set as a barrier, and don't be held back by what you've accomplished before as though it is your high-water mark. It's not. You can push it higher. You can go farther.

If you innovate with a vision of what could and should be, success will happen along the way. And if you can follow even a few of these guidelines, you don't have to be a rocket scientist to do what Elon Musk has done, if albeit on a smaller scale. You can learn from his principles and the story of how he combined different trends, and you can have similar results in categories in your life.

KEY INSIGHTS, KEY SHIFTS

I'm dangerous enough to code and sociable enough to sell our company, and…that's a deadly combination in entrepreneurship.

—KEVIN SYSTROM

In 2006 Kevin Systrom, a senior at Stanford University, was offered a job from a guy named Mark Zuckerberg. He was to help build a photo sharing service for what was then called "the Facebook." Systrom turned it down. "Working at a start-up and making a lot of money was never a thing," he said. "That's why I decided to just finish up school."

Systrom was a B student, even though he worked hard at school. He was studying computer science, but it was tough for him. He ended up switching to easier subjects like engineering and management. To study photography, he took a trip to Italy where he fell in love with vintage photo techniques, using specialty filters on lenses so the photographs would look antique.

He also found an interest in entrepreneurship. Systrom had spent some of his free time building websites. One was called Photobox, which his fraternity used to post pictures of their keg parties.

He eventually entered Stanford's elite Mayfield Fellows Program, which takes a select group of entrepreneurial students and pairs them with start-up entrepreneurs in Silicon Valley. The students learn about the basics of starting up a company firsthand—funding and venture capital, hiring and acquiring talent, building solid business plans, etc.

Through this program, Systrom took on a summer internship at a place called Odeo. Odeo eventually turned into Twitter, but it was a podcast company at the time. He was able to make some great connections with Twitter founders Ev Williams and Jack Dorsey, who turned out to be influential entrepreneurs.

When Systrom graduated from Stanford, he was offered a six-figure job at Microsoft. He turned it down. Instead, he hired on at Google for quite a bit less because he thought there might be more long-term opportunity there. For many people in the tech field, Google is a dream job. However, the job simply bored Systrom, so he quit.

IN SILICON VALLEY THEY CALL IT BEING A "BROGRAMMER"—ONE OF THE BROTHERHOOD OF PROGRAMMERS.

His next adventure was to work at a travel start-up. It

was there that he grew his skill as a programmer. In Silicon Valley they call it being a "brogrammer"—one of the brotherhood of programmers. Programing was a critical skill for Systrom to put it all together. "All of a sudden," he said, "I had a new skill I could put to use. When you had an idea, you could actually create it." And this was a guy who definitely had ideas.

He had the idea to create a company that would provide a website for photos, location check-ins, and social gaming. There were competitors in a similar space, like Zynga and Foursquare. Systrom had an idea to combine the elements in a unique way into a company he would call Burbn. He found start-up venture capital, but he needed a cofounder, so he went looking for candidates.

Back at Stanford, Systrom had made quite a few connections, and one of them was a guy named Mike Krieger. It took some convincing, but eventually Systrom convinced Krieger to come work for him. On Krieger's first day, Systrom walked in and stated, "Burbn won't work." Can you imagine being recruited to a new company, dropping everything you were doing, and showing up, excited to get going, and the guy who just hired you comes in and says the whole thing just won't work? But as they thought about it, it was clear the competitors had become too entrenched in the space. Systrom and Krieger were too far behind.

So they made a key shift. They decided to drop the location check-in feature, and then discarded the social gaming aspect. That left the focus solely on the photo sharing. This shift turned out to make all the difference.

The shift was accompanied by a key insight. The iPhone was fairly new at this point, and its adoption into people's lives was creating new behaviors. "It was the opportunity to create a new type of service. A social network that wasn't based on a computer, but based on the computer in your hand." They were some of the first entrepreneurs to realize that the iPhone had changed the world.

They realized the tech world had been split in two. At some point in the past, the Internet had changed the way people do many things, including business. In the dotcom boom, a rush of businesses realized the Internet represented a new way of doing business. That rush became a frenzy. With the advent of the iPhone, Android devices, and other smart phone technology, there was a second phase—the Internet was now mobile.

If you travel to other countries, especially less developed ones, you'll notice that most people aren't on the Internet at their home computers. They may not even have electricity coming to their house. But they have smartphones and are connected to the Internet on their mobile devices. The idea of Internet on a computer is almost foreign in many places. It's old-fashioned. The way much of the world thinks about the Internet is that it's in your hand.

Systrom and Krieger's key insight was that the tech world had been split into computer-based and mobile Internet access. Mobile had the momentum. They were among the first to build something directly for it. They built what's called a natively mobile social networking service. This key shift and key insight created a billion-dollar company.

The app they created was designed from the beginning to work on a mobile device. The pictures and content would be generated and captured on the mobile, and then pictures and content would be shared right from the device. The cameras on mobile devices have only gotten better since the first ones, so this just made sense.

It was a brilliant idea, a key distinction, just a tiny hair-split of an idea that others didn't see. But somehow Systrom and Krieger saw it.

Peter Thiel, the tech guru who cofounded PayPal, said the way to create a monopoly is to carve out a new space. When you do something no one else is doing, there is no competition. He wrote about how companies like Google can have free food in their cafeterias and all these massive employee perks because they're not competing in the marketplace. They effectively got to a marketplace that didn't exist before and hogged it. When you own the space, there are massive profits to be made, and you can do whatever you want with it.

When everyone is stuck competing for market space in something that has already been defined, it's been called a "red ocean." All the sharks are feeding there — it's crowded, and there is blood in the water. A "blue ocean" describes a market where you are the only player. It's not bloody because you, the only one there, can dominate without the struggle. Peter Theil called creating your own niche the "zero to one" concept, and it's effectively what Systrom and Krieger did. They were natively mobile before most people realized the significance of mobile or even that it was distinct.

Systrom and Krieger went to work programming a photo app they called "Code Name." Krieger worked on the Apple IOS software side of it, and Systrom worked on the back-end code. The process took them just a couple of weeks, with both of them coding like crazy toward this great idea. When they were done with it, though, neither of them was very enthusiastic about what they had built.

Frustrated, Systrom took a break. He rented a cheap little bungalow in Mexico on the ocean and took a step back. He felt he had misfired on the Code Name app. It was just not that cool. They had launched it and shared it with a couple of friends, but it wasn't a big deal.

He was walking the beach with his girlfriend, and she had her smartphone out, asking him about a picture that one of their friends had taken with the Code Name app. "How did she get it to look so cool?" she asked. "I like that effect. It kind of looks old."

Systrom had studied vintage photography in college, of course, and he nonchalantly answered that it was a filter. The friend had put a filter on his camera. Then it hit him. Filters! The vacation was over, and he got out his laptop and coded nonstop, building the first filter to integrate into their app.

If you've used photo apps, you know that once you have a picture on there, you can put different effects and filters on the picture. Back when the phone cameras weren't as good, these effects and filters hid the fact that the photo wasn't such high quality. The system created all kinds of filters to enhance the pictures people were taking on their smartphones.

Systrom had fallen upon a key combination. The decision to get away from his work for a while had paid off. Sometimes a little break in the action, a chance to let your brain soak a little bit, pays big dividends. Sometimes you are simply trying too hard; you just need to let it go a little, and the genius will come through.

They renamed the app Instagram and shared it with some of their friends and connections. Of course, Systrom had great connections from Stanford and from his entrepreneur program there. When Jack Dorsey at Twitter—who has more Twitter followers than anybody—tweets about your new photo app, that's pretty good free exposure.

The buzz began to build around Instagram. They had made it easy to take input from a mobile device and post it while mobile. They had taken a page out of Steve Jobs's playbook. Make it easy. Make it slick. Make it cool. Jobs had proved that that combination was a winner.

They launched Instagram on the Apple store on October 6, 2010. There were 25,000 downloads of the app in the first twenty-four hours. "From that day on," Systrom said, "we never had the same life." After a month they had a million users.

Now they had different kinds of problems. They worked feverishly behind the scenes to keep the app running;

photos involve a huge amount of data, and it's a lot to hold and manage electronically. They had few employees, so the cofounders and just a couple other people had to handle everything.

Stories are told of the two cofounders and the employees having to have computers on them everywhere they went. When a person joined their team, he or she had to agree they would have a laptop on them at all times because the company never knew when something was going to go down and need attention. One time an employee was at a farm-fresh dinner event, and he was trying to find a place where he could get a clear wireless signal. The only place that worked was near the chicken coop, so he sat there with the farmer's chickens fixing the app.

In September 2012, Facebook bought Instagram, just twenty-two months after that moment on the beach. The price was $1 billion. Systrom was going to work at Facebook after all.

At the time of the purchase, many experts said the deal represented the kind of overexuberance that had been seen in the dotcom bubble. In the time since, however, it is looking more as if Facebook got a great deal. They got Systrom and Krieger, after all, who still work there, and Instagram is now estimated to be worth an incredible $10 billion.

Author Steve Bertoni notes that Instagram, with its 200 million active users, was a cheap way for Facebook and Zuckerberg to jump into the mobile game. Because

Instagram had carved out that new market space, they became valuable quickly, and Facebook realized that.

The story is amazing. A hardworking kid who had a bit of trouble getting computer engineering in school figured out a way to make it work. Systrom succeeded in creating a breakthrough product.

There are three keys to a breakthrough (a key insight, a key combination, and a key shift), and the founding of Instagram presents a great example that anyone in any business can learn from and duplicate. You may not form a billion-dollar business (then again, you might), but you can have a breakthrough if you have these keys.

MINDSET MEMOS

1. Key Insight

At Instagram, the initial insight was to create a product from which you could view friends' photos of their adventures and see where they were at the time. The main key insight, though, was that mobile was where it was at. If the user could generate a picture on his mobile device and then share it on his mobile device, that would create a new experience that everyone adopting mobile technology would want to experience.

A key insight is when you realize there is either a problem to be fixed or something totally cool to do that hasn't been done. Dropbox, for instance, was founded by a guy named Drew Houston. He was riding a bus home from work when he realized he had forgotten his thumb drive containing data on it for a project he was working on. He found himself wishing there were some way to access the data he had left behind. That was his key insight — that there ought to be a way to access data from anywhere and from any device. That had never been done, and it was Houston's opportunity.

2. Key Combination

A key combination is when you put two things together in a way that has not been done before. For Instagram this combination came when Systrom realized that including filters for the photo app would create an interesting and creative experience. There had been people who had put filters on the photos from their mobile devices, but Instagram figured out how to make it work seamlessly.

The question you should ask yourself if you want a breakthrough in your business is this: "What new combination can I make that has never been done, or can I do it in a way no one has ever done before?"

Dropbox's key combination came when Houston realized that not only would people want to access their own data, but they would want to share it as well. Until Dropbox, it was difficult to get large files to someone without physically transporting them on a thumb drive. That combination of convenient data access and the ability to share it was powerful.

3. Key Shift

Any major breakthrough also contains a key shift. A shift is a slight adjustment in trajectory, setting your sights in a slightly different configuration than you have before. At Instagram, the shift occurred when they realized that Foursquare had too much traction in the market ahead of them, so they needed to streamline Burbn down into something simpler and more original.

A shift often asks, "What could be simplified? How do we take just a little better aim at the target?" Sometimes a slight adjustment is all that is needed. But other times it looks more like a complete overhaul.

For Dropbox, the key shift was centered on how to get people to adopt the new technology. Even though the central data storage and sharing idea made it easier, old habits die hard. Their key shift came when they realized they should just offer people some storage for free. If you give away five megabytes of storage for free, pretty soon people will see the value of the model and want ten megabytes. People tend to acquire more and more data and still want to have access to that data. This way of doing business has been dubbed the "freemium" model. You give some away for free, and if they like your product, many people will pay for more.

4. Putting It Together

Any company or person you see innovating in a big way will likely demonstrate this formula of a key insight, key combination, and key shift. What could yours be? What are your skills, talents, or resources, and how could you think about or combine them in a novel way to create more value? Maybe you need to acquire a new skill like Systrom did in order to take full advantage of a skill or talent that you already have.

KINDLING
A FIRE

*I believe you have to be willing to be
misunderstood if you're going to innovate.*[2]
—JEFF BEZOS

In 2003, the e-book was dead. Jeff Bezos and Amazon
had passed on the idea. Barnes and Noble had partnered
a few years earlier with a company called NuvoMedia
to produce the Rocketbook. They sold twenty thousand
of them in a year. But the dotcom bubble had burst, and
things were uncertain in the tech market, so NuvoMedia
was sold. Eventually, the company went defunct. Even
good ideas can die if the market isn't ready for them.

Of course, the e-book wouldn't stay dead. In 2004,
Amazon's Bezos launched a secret project called Lab 126.
The number "1" stood for the letter "A" and the "26"
stood for the letter "Z." Bezos' vision for Amazon from
the beginning was for the company to be the "everything"
store. His first dream in that process was that Amazon

would carry every book ever written anywhere at any time. So it was time to bring the e-book back.

Bezos instructed Lab 126 that they were to "Disrupt Amazon's own successful bookselling business with an e-book device of some kind." Bezos understood the importance of e-books and had not acted on the idea earlier only because it wasn't something he could have controlled. Amazon, looking to the future, could see the huge potential of digital media. The company had other problems to get through at the time, so they didn't pick it up right away. But things change.

In April 2003 Apple had unveiled its iTunes music store. Steve Jobs had been working in secret, speaking to music label presidents, record company owners, and recording artists of all kinds, talking them into contributing their music for sale at $0.99 per song download. The iPod was already out there, so the stage was set. Music piracy was also a hot issue at this time, with services such as Napster helping people basically steal music. The music industry was a bit on edge, uncertain how they would deal with this challenge.

Jobs realized he had the answer. He could make downloads easy and inexpensive, and people could then load them onto their cool new iPods that had just been released the year before. Most people didn't know this revolutionary music service was coming. Jobs persuaded most of the music industry to put their music on the iTunes store. The store was an immediate sensation. Suddenly, Apple, which had not even been in the music business, was the world's largest distributor of music. The people at Amazon were caught off guard.

Bezos' company sold CDs and was a bit taken aback by the sudden competitor. Jobs's love for music had driven him to solve the music distribution problem. Bezos' love of books would drive him to do the same thing with books. Author Brad Stone commented, "If Amazon was to continue to thrive as a bookseller in a new digital age, it must own the e-book business in the same way that Apple now controlled the music business."[3] Lab 126 was tasked with the solution to digital books. Diego Piecentini, an executive at Amazon, put it this way: "It's far better to cannibalize yourself than to have someone else do it."[38]

Basically, they didn't want to be Kodak. Kodak made film in the heyday of film camera technology. Of course, digital technology came along and completely killed off the film camera business. The funny thing is, Kodak itself invented the digital camera. You will notice that not a person today owns a Kodak digital camera or a Kodak smartphone, and yet they pioneered the technology.

Kodak realized that digital was a destructive technology and that it would kill their wildly profitable film business. They didn't want to push it. Unfortunately for Kodak, digital photography was also an inevitable technology, and they allowed competitors not only to get ahead of them in digital cameras but also to drive them out of the film market as well. Amazon wanted to avoid a similar fate.

Bezos announced to his staff that they would develop their own dedicated electronic reading device. As we think of Amazon today, they are not just a bookstore — among other things, they are a comprehensive online marketplace. Back in 2004, though, they were pretty much a bookstore that sold other items as well.

To many of Amazon's top executives, this e-book strategy sounded insane. It was way outside the company's core competencies, and it was a costly enterprise. One insider, Jeff Wilke, said, "I thought it would be difficult and disruptive, and I was skeptical that it was the right use of our resources. It turned out that most of the things I predicted would happen actually happened, and we still powered through it because Jeff is not deterred by short-term setbacks."[39]

Bezos championed the e-reader idea with fervor. Everyone else only saw the difficulties and obstacles. Bezos likely saw those obstacles as well, but he also saw the vision for the new technology. He wanted Amazon to become for books what Apple had become for music, and to do that, he had to control the entire customer experience. Amazon would seek to be part of every stage of book buying, from the moment the customer wanted to buy a book, through looking for a book to buy, finding a book, buying it, downloading it to the e-reader and flipping through the pages, all the way to reaching the last word on the last page.

Amazon also wanted to make the process simple and intuitive. They wanted it simple enough that a grandmother who couldn't program a VCR could figure out how to buy an e-book from Amazon.com, put it on her e-reader, and read it with absolutely no problems. Bezos wanted sleek hardware, great design, simplicity, ease of use, convenience, a smooth digital e-book store, and an intuitive interface. That was all. No problem, right?

Of course, Amazon had never manufactured anything. They were a retailer that was supposedly going to make these amazing electronic devices. Bezos figured that since they didn't have the talent to do that, they would simply hire the talent.

Either the plan was crazy, or Jeff Bezos was a genius. Those who bought into the vision at Amazon became known as Jeff-Bots. These were people who were going to follow through on the crazy plan regardless of appearances and problems.

One of the powerful Jeff-Bots at Amazon was a technologist named Steve Kessel. Kessel had worked at Amazon for a long time and had become one of the top performers. He was in charge of both the physical and electronic books at Amazon at the time.

In 2004, Bezos took Kessel into his office and gave him one clear assignment. He was to be solely in charge of the digital book business. Bezos figured that Amazon could no longer afford to have one person over both divisions. The person who was going to bring this e-book vision to life would need to be totally dedicated and tenacious. Kessel was told, "Your job is to kill your own business."[40]

Most people resist change. It's a natural human reaction. They get comfortable with one idea of how things should be done and simply don't want to bother with anything new or possibly better. It takes a good deal of courage to create a division of your own company dedicated to the destruction of the rest of it. Some call this "creative destruction." In this case, it was self-imposed creative destruction. They were willing to sacrifice what they were to become something better — something that would survive the future technological shift and help them remain competitive.

> IT TAKES A GOOD DEAL OF COURAGE TO CREATE A DIVISION OF YOUR OWN COMPANY DEDICATED TO THE DESTRUCTION OF THE REST OF IT.

This is a good idea not only for business but also for people. We should be willing to make the changes that will transform who we are — sacrifice who we are for something better. Instead, most people entrench and protect and dig in to resist change. Perhaps you know people like this. They are not growing and certainly not willing to destroy what is good in their lives in order to get something great.

Kessel asked Bezos about the time line for the project. The answer was that they were already late. They needed to start yesterday. There is power in having not quite enough time. There is magic in having not enough time to think about things too much but just enough to get going. Having abundant time to accomplish a big goal is dangerous because it's too easy to procrastinate. Meanwhile, time flies by. and you get in the trap of inaction.

If you put a time line on a big goal that feels a little tight and creates a little bit of anxiety, you then look at that time line and think, "Uh-oh. I don't think that's quite enough to get it done." This is not hurry, but enough of a squeeze that you aren't distracted by little things that can take your focus away. As Pat Riley said, "The main thing is to keep the main thing the main thing." The press of time can help facilitate that focus.

One engineer on the e-reader project said, "We were told to do one thing with maniacal focus." Many people could use this idea in their own lives. Instead of being all over the place, what would happen if

"WE WERE TOLD TO DO ONE THING WITH MANIACAL FOCUS."

they took the most important part of their lives or businesses and concentrated on that part with maniacal focus?

Amazon took some of the brightest people it could find and put them in a separate building in a different town removed from the rest of the company where they wouldn't get distracted or leak secrets. They had just this one thing to focus on—making this world-class device that met Bezos' vision. All that talent focused with the intensity of a short time line—this was Lab 126.

The Amazon e-reader was a totally different concept from the Rocketbook, which had represented more of an "Oh well, we'll try it and see what happens" approach. Amazon's effort was comprehensive but also focused on simplicity. Bezos wanted people to be able to download any book, anywhere, any time, and also at one price.

Bezos also made one more simple but critical innovation. He didn't want customers to be forced to hook the device to their computer in order to download a book onto it. For him, that was too cumbersome and inconvenient. It doesn't sound like that big a deal to have to sit down at your computer and hook up a cord — thirty seconds and your download is ready. But Bezos had a different vision. "I want to be able to be hustling through an airport, late for a flight, realize I don't have a book, get on Amazon.com and in just a few seconds, a few keystrokes, it's on my thing and I can read it on the plane...I want anybody to be able to do that anywhere, any time, any book."[7]

To Bezos, this one insight drove the whole project. For some reason, it just occurred to him as the critical piece. He received pushback on this idea. Engineers and network specialists basically said the costs would outweigh the benefits and that it couldn't possibly be done. Bezos could have easily caved on this, but he absolutely insisted that it had to be that way.

He argued that the process of configuring the device to work with Wi-Fi networks was too complicated for the nontechnical customers. In 2004, Wi-Fi was not quite as ubiquitous as it is today. You expect your grandmother to be providing Wi-Fi these days, but ten years ago she didn't know what Wi-Fi was.

For Bezos, it had to be cellular connectivity — anywhere, all the time, any book, any time. His solution was to build cellular connectivity right into the hardware. No data plans, no cell subscription, no monthly cost, no contracts — it would just be on there. The user wouldn't have to know anything about it.

Brad Stone wrote, "Bezos insisted that customers should never have to know the wireless connection was there or even pay for the access."[41] When he was told by employees that it wouldn't work and would cost too much, Bezos basically told them that their job was to figure it out. Bezos would worry about how to make it work from a business perspective.

The top secret effort encountered all kinds of problems and delays. Two of the biggest suppliers of the technology for the device sued each other, and the court got involved and locked them down so they couldn't ship. The designers would try to cut corners just to make something feasible, but Bezos wouldn't go for it. They tried to complicate the device, and he sent them back to the drawing board. The process ended up taking some time as they ironed everything out. Bezos was once asked how much resource and money he would spend on the project. His answer was "How much do we have?"[42]

Another enormous challenge was to get publishers to agree to sell their books for the new device. Steve Jobs had convinced record labels to get on board with the iTunes store, but Bezos didn't have many contacts in the publishing world. You would think that, being the biggest bookseller in the world, he would have been well connected there, but that wasn't the case. He had to send out his minions to convince the booksellers that the e-book was the future of books. They didn't agree.

Some of them said, "We have seen this before. Someone has already done that, and it didn't work." But Bezos was undaunted and determined that somehow he would convince publishers. They set a goal to have a hundred thousand e-books for sale on the day the device would launch. At the time that goal was set, only about twenty thousand books had been digitized in the entire world. Yet Bezos wanted five times that amount, and he wanted them within two years!

Amazon had already had some skirmishes with publishers. For one thing, publishers disliked the idea of reader reviews being available to people looking to buy books. Studies show that when people are passionate enough about a book to review it, they are more likely to write negative reviews. The publishers believed negative reviews would harm sales.

Another complaint publishers had was that Amazon allowed third parties to sell on their site. Amazon had built a huge selling platform, and they let other people sell used books from their site. Publishers disliked this because a book that sold for $30 new would be seen on the site alongside a used book offered by an independent seller for perhaps $6. There were several other issues as well that the publishers and Amazon had disagreed about in the past, so Amazon didn't have the best relationship with them.

Now Amazon had to convince these same publishers to take the bet on e-books, even though e-books didn't have a great record so far. And while Amazon was trying to convince publishers, they were still trying to keep the project secret. So Amazon's pitch to the publishers was basically, "We need you to spend thirty grand each digitizing about 80 percent of your titles." When the publishers objected that e-books had been tried before and that it hadn't worked — and pointed out that Amazon was an online bookseller and had nothing apparently new that would make it work — Amazon couldn't even counter by telling them about the new device they were working on.

One Amazon employee said of this period, "I describe my job as dragging publishers kicking and screaming into the twenty-first century." Bezos' odd, genius conviction that the device had to be seamlessly wireless was the final piece that broke the logjam. As soon as Amazon decided to reveal a little of what they were doing, some of the first big publishers "saw it" immediately and jumped on board.

That ability to provide the customer with instant gratification by way of the ability to download a book any time they wanted, anywhere they wanted, was convincing. Bezos' insistence that the device be constantly online and in connection with the online bookstore had paid off. It turned out to be the deal maker.

It took some arm twisting as well as convincing. If a publisher resisted supplying books digitally for Amazon, then that publisher's books simply wouldn't show up on the search page. You could search for authors for those resistant publishers, and they simply wouldn't come up on the Amazon search engine. This would affect the book sales for those publishers by double-digit percentages. Before long, the publishers came around. All of a sudden the e-book idea started to sound pretty good.

Perhaps that was a little heavy-handed. Sometimes a little fear is needed, though, to get the job done. Digital books were the obvious future, and the industry was too comfortable with what was being done. They didn't have the same piracy fear as the recording companies did when they agreed to work with Jobs. Bezos had to become the bogeyman himself to get it done. He played the role well.

Even at that, the launch was delayed for over a year. Some design fixes that were required, and Bezos remained committed to the goal of a hundred thousand e-books. Even if it meant delays, they would stick to that goal. The date was etched in sand but the goal cut in stone.

One more hurdle for the publishing industry was Bezos' pricing strategy. He wanted all the books across the board to be priced at $9.99. This threw the publishers for yet another loop. They had done the digitizing and come along kicking and screaming, and then Amazon asked them to sell at a significantly discounted price. It was too late for them to back out—they were already in. The $9.99 price became the standard for the industry, however reluctantly.

On November 19, 2007, Jeff Bezos walked out onto a stage and announced the Kindle to the world. Its development had taken over three years, massive investment, and the hard work of a diligent and innovative team. It had required Bezos championing the concept through every step of development. The Kindle weighed about ten ounces, could carry two hundred titles, had an E-Ink screen that was easy on the eyes, and had that critical Whispernet connectivity — the ability to seamlessly buy just about any book, any time, any place.

One of the Jeff-Bots, a guy named Russ Grandeinetti, said, "I think the reason Kindle succeeded while others failed is that we were obsessive. Not about trying to build the sexiest gadget in the world, but rather about building something that actually fulfilled what people wanted."[4] The original batch of twenty-five thousand Kindles sold out within a couple of hours. This presented a bit of a problem, since Bezos was flying around the world making speeches about the device, and customers couldn't actually get one. Amazon couldn't make them fast enough.

The Kindle gained momentum with the release of the Kindle 2 in early 2009 with many improvements. Amazon has since sold millions and millions of Kindles. The company doesn't release exact sales numbers, but billions of dollars' worth of Kindle devices and e-books are sold per year, and their e-book business now matches their physical book business. You could call it resounding success, from which there is much to learn.

MINDSET MEMOS

1. Do one thing with maniacal focus.

Pick what is important to you, and go for it with "maniacal focus."

Consider your professional life or your business. What is the one great thing that you could do with maniacal focus? What is the one thing you could really pour yourself into?

2. Be willing to kill your own business.

Harry S. Dent talks about the "s curve" concept where in the beginning, everybody thinks your new idea is stupid and they run from it. Next, the idea is adopted by a few. Finally, everybody has to have it. The e-reader phenomenon seems obvious now, but it didn't seem obvious back in the early 2000s.

Be looking for the changes necessary in your industry, and be willing to sacrifice what is good now for what will be great in the future. Innovate in order to compete.

3. Press on regardless of opposition.

You may have to fight to bring even your own key constituents along. Sometimes, when you know you are right, you might have to bring people along kicking and screaming. That's what leadership sometimes requires.

4. There are times when you have to hire your way to the right talent.

There is no substitute for having the right people on your team. You just have to find those right people. You can't get blood from a stone, and if you're going to make something magnificent, you have to have a team of excellent performers. Learn to attract top talent to your cause. Good leadership almost always involves effective recruiting.

5. Use your creativity to build what you want in your life and business.

You must have passion in order to do something really great. Bring into existence what you want to see happen in an area you love. Bezos loved books and brought about the e-reader. Jobs loved music and brought the system of digitized music into reality. What do you love? What needs to be created in order to make it better?

6. Find others who buy into your vision.

Find some Jeff-Bots. Find people who buy in in a big way and are willing to go to great lengths to help bring about your vision. By the way, those Jeff-Bots at Amazon are now multimillionaires with stock options and great jobs at one of the largest companies in the world. Not a bad reward for buying into Bezos' ideas. Success in life is often a result of the leaders we choose to follow.

7. Simple is the key.

Never stop thinking about how you can refine and simplify what you do to make it better. Simple is not easy, but it is worth it.

8. An overriding goal drives decision and maintains focus.

Somehow the everything-store concept finally got Jeff Bezos to dig in and invest in the e-book concept. His goal for constant and universal connectivity then drove the project to completion, and this goal brought the publishing world along as well.

9. Give the customers what they want.

You have to be obsessed with the customer side of what you do. How does your product or service feel to him? How easy is it for her to digest? How easy is it for him to figure out what you're trying to accomplish? How easy is it for her to trust what you're doing? How simple is it for them to make the next big purchase? Understand exactly what your customer's experience is, and make it the best it can be.

10. Even if you have the formula just right, you might not be an overnight sensation.

Although Amazon sold those first twenty-five thousand units in an hour and had trouble keeping up with demand, the Kindle wasn't a clear runaway success. It wasn't until Kindle 2 came out that it really started to take off. Sometimes you can have everything in place and still release to the sound of crickets.

The iPod wasn't an overnight success either. Sales were slow the first year, and Apple thought they had somehow botched it. They almost went back to the drawing board to reconsider the spin wheel control because they thought they had perhaps made it too simple. When the iTunes store was launched, the iPod really took off. The store was the missing piece that made everything work.

Be ready to face a little uncertainty and just press on, because even if you have it just right, your enterprise might not take off right away.

11. Leverage what you have to get what you want.

Amazon used the prominent product placement of the Kindle on their established bookselling website to promote the Kindle. They also used their size and prominence in the bookselling industry to coerce publishers to adopt the digital revolution.

You, too, have resources. You have things you've accomplished, a network of people. You have credibility and clout you can leverage to get from where you are to where you want to go. Take what you've built, and use it to get what you want.

12. Keep improving your masterpiece, even after it's been released.

Even when you hit a goal, go ahead and start running immediately to hit something even better. When you have built something, get to work building it to be even better. Don't rest on your laurels. Improvement is a never-ending task.

13. Genius inspires genius.

The less of a genius you are, the more you need geniuses around you. The more of a genius you are, the more it will bring out the genius in those around you. The formula is the same. Place yourself around genius, and see if two heads aren't better than one. Two heads are probably more like ten heads and ten heads are probably more like two hundred.

Find people who will bring out the best in you. Find people who make your ideas grow and get better when you are around them.

14. Missing goals is okay.

You can reset the date on goals and it's okay. The greatest projects that have ever been completed weren't done exactly on time, but they were done because someone didn't allow a missed goal to cause them to give up. The initial goal pushed them, but when they didn't meet the time line, they just reset the date and kept on going. Set your goals in stone and their dates in sand.

CHAPTER

8

CREATIVE COMBINATIONS

If you want volume, you have to bring breakthrough value, either some kind of new efficiency, or... something previously unavailable.

—HAL SPERLICH

Stories of leadership and success are scattered throughout history and the business world. We can learn much from these stories by identifying the principles and examining the mindset of the most effective leaders. Sometimes such inspiring stories are found in less obvious places. What, for instance, could be inspiring about the story behind the origin of the minivan?

The minivan has the reputation of being one of the least sexy cars on the market. This is the car you drive when you need to cart around a load of kids or provide a shuttle service. On the other hand, it has been a major part of American suburbia for more than thirty years. It's easy to take that kind of impact for granted, but the story of how it came to be is worth looking into.

For the story of the minivan, we have to go all the way back to a car called the Edsel. Ford's Edsel was one of the great failures in automotive history. The car was such a grand flop that the name became a euphemism for a total failure of design—a product that was dead on arrival. Ford had released the car with high expectations but very little market research, and it fell flat as an unqualified disaster.

Learning from its mistakes, by the early 1960s, Ford had a twenty-person staff devoted solely to market research. Lee Iacocca, a Ford corporate fast-tracker, said, "We have experts who watch for every change in the customer's pulse beat. For a long time now, we have been aware that an unprecedented youth boom was in the making."[45]

> "WE HAVE EXPERTS WHO WATCH FOR EVERY CHANGE IN THE CUSTOMER'S PULSE BEAT."
> —LEE IACOCCA

The Baby Boomers had arrived in the early sixties. The number of Americans between the ages of fifteen and nineteen increased by 41 percent in the decade. The number of Americans between the ages of twenty and twenty-four jumped 54 percent. In the early sixties, most of these Boomers were looking to buy their first car. Only 21 percent of households had more than one car at the time, but that was rapidly changing. Nowadays, very few households have only one car. It's hard to imagine, but back in that time few women drove; they relied on their husbands to drive. However, into the sixties, more and more women were owning and driving cars.

With these demographic shifts, more people started driving than ever, and the automotive industry boomed, along with the general economy. In 1960, John F. Kennedy became the youngest man ever elected US president, and that seemed appropriate for the time's massive youth movement.

Two young guys, who would leave an indelible mark, were working for Ford at this time. One of them was Hal Sperlich. At thirty-one years old, he was a vice president and product planner. The other was Lee Iacocca, who was the youngest head up to that time of the Ford Division at Ford Motor Company. He had come up through the company as a salesman and worked his way to the top — not the usual path for an executive.

These guys were smart enough to cater to the youth wave with the perfect car for the time, the Ford Mustang. The car fit the youth movement vibe perfectly. It wasn't actually named after the horse, originally. The Mustang was actually named after the P-51 warplane that had been famous toward the end of World War II.

The Mustang wasn't an entirely new vehicle. Ford had designed it on the same platform as a previous car, the Falcon. For the Mustang, they converted this platform into a sporty two-door coupe. It was a great design. Some said it looked like it was moving even when it was sitting still. It incorporated the old Falcon engine and a lot of Falcon parts, but overall it was a great combination of the old and new. The car was stylish but modestly priced. There were a huge amount of possible upgrades, with over forty specific options you could choose from. The Mustang was a huge success.

Hal Sperlich, this young upstart who was one of the geniuses behind the Mustang, had another idea for something he code-named the Mini Max. (He was arguably better at designing cars than naming them.) His idea was that the car would be of minimal length so it would fit into the average garage, but it would have maximum space inside. Basically, it was the early concept of the minivan.

Sperlich took this idea to his boss, Henry Ford II (Henry Ford's grandson), who flatly rejected the idea. Sperlich saw promise in the Mini Max concept, however, so he kept working on it and brought it back a second time to his boss. The idea was rejected again. Sperlich just kept trying, though. Any time he could get the ear of Henry Ford II, he would talk up the Mini Max idea.

At some point Ford had had enough of Sperlich's persistence. He called Iacocca into his office and told him to fire Sperlich. Iacocca reminded Ford that this was one of their most valuable leaders and the guy behind the wildly successful Mustang. Ford simply didn't like Sperlich, though, and Iacocca was forced to fire him. Sperlich then got a job over at Chrysler, which was happy to have him.

After a couple months, Ford fired Iacocca as well. When the papers asked why he fired two successful and seemingly key employees, Ford flatly responded with something to the effect of "Sometimes you don't like someone, and that's it." It didn't matter to him that these two men had been a major part of one of the most successful cars Ford had ever produced. Ford was the kind of boss who would remind people his name was on the building.

So Iacocca, at fifty-three years old, was looking for a job, and Sperlich, over at Chrysler, decided to recruit him. Chrysler wasn't doing well at the time. In fact, if there had been a heart monitor on the company, it would have shown pretty much a flat line. They would have been calling for the paddles. Iacocca said later that if he had had the slightest idea what lay ahead with Chrysler, he wouldn't have gone there for all the money in the world. He was hired on as the president of Chrysler Motors in 1978. Within a year, he was named CEO and chairman.

Essentially, he was given the whole company and tasked with the seemingly impossible job of fixing it. Chrysler was in serious trouble. They had a cash flow crunch, massive excess inventory, and cars that wouldn't sell except to rental fleets. They tried to get loans, but banks were just not risking any more money on them. Chrysler's answer was to try to get a loan guarantee from the government. Basically, they were asking the government to be their cosigner. Chrysler was like a teenager trying to get their Uncle Sam to sign on a loan. If you have ever had a teenager try to get you to cosign on a loan, you know that this is not generally a good idea. The government refused to guarantee a loan, and in June 1979, Chrysler ran out of money and couldn't pay their suppliers. This meant they were just about done, but at the last minute, Lee Iacocca secured a loan directly from the US government. That's no big deal now, but back then it was unprecedented.

Chrysler wasn't all bad. They had a few things going for them. For one, Chrysler now had some good leaders. Also, they had come upon some valuable technology by accident. Sperlich had discovered that Chrysler owned a European subsidiary named Simca. They had to sell the company because they needed the money, but Sperlich was shrewd and bought the rights to a piece of technology that Simca had developed, and it turned out to be a major key in our story of the minivan: the technology of front-wheel drive.

With Iacocca achieving the feat of putting Chrysler on firmer ground financially, and with Sperlich discovering and recognizing the significance of front-wheel drive technology, things began to turn around. With front-wheel drive you can have a smaller engine because you don't have to run a driveshaft to the back of the car. You don't have to have a hump in the middle of the car, so you can have more room to work with in the interior. You can turn the engine sideways to create more room. Chrysler produced a couple of tiny cars, the Dodge Omni and the Plymouth Horizon, which were basically the same car under different brands.

The timing for these new small cars was perfect because in 1979, there was the Iran hostage situation and a terrible economy. Gas prices shot through the roof. These smaller cars got excellent gas mileage for the time, and they sold well. Sperlich had his second great victory and for the second time had produced the perfect car at the perfect time.

Sperlich and Iacocca then used this same front-wheel drive technology to produce a couple of sedans. Because of the smaller engine and lack of the need for the driveshaft, they were smaller sedans than had been produced, but they felt bigger inside and were decent on gas. They came to be known as K cars, the Dodge Aires and the Plymouth Reliant. Launched in 1981, they were wildly successful. Chrysler sold more than 300,000 of them that first year. That set them up for their third great automotive victory.

Enter the minivan. The idea that Ford had rejected was now resurrected at Chrysler. Sperlich set his sights again toward his Mini Max idea. Iacocca was supportive. However, as had happened at Ford, hardly anyone else at Chrysler could see it, and almost everybody was against it.

At the time the paradigm was that you either made cars or trucks. Vans were more or less the odd man out. They were fine for plumbers to work out of, for churches to cart people to services, or for people with unusually large families, but they weren't seen as an idea that would have wide appeal. The carmakers didn't want to build them, and the truck people saw them as a wimpy niche vehicle and were more interested in making trucks, which they knew would sell well.

Sperlich found himself opposed yet again. It makes you wonder how many touchdowns this guy needed to score before someone would trust him with the ball. What did he have to do to prove that he knew what he was doing?

The vehicle Sperlich proposed was a truck-like vehicle on a car chassis. It would be light, maneuverable, easy to drive, have tons of room inside, have a high seating position, and great gas mileage. All of this was made possible by the front-wheel drive tech that had spurred Chrysler's renaissance. Paul Ingrassia wrote, "The man who built the Mustang on the platform of the Falcon wanted to build his new van on the platform of the K car."[46]

Sperlich had learned his lesson, though, and he didn't go on a pestering campaign to try to force the issue. He could have simply rammed the idea through, but he wanted people to buy in. He wanted people to catch the vision of this new type of vehicle. So he tried a novel approach—a way of helping people see the error of their thinking without confrontation. He wrote a satirical letter and sent it to all the engineers.

His letter was written from the point of view of the fictional president of a fictional company. This fictional company was in the business of making minivans, and in the letter the fictional president was responding to an engineer who had suggested that sedans were a much better way to go. The president makes the case for the minivan. Why would you want to take that large spacious area in the back and just make a trunk out of it? Why would you want to cram the kids all together and have them bite and kick and scratch each other when they could all have room the way they did in the minivan?

The letter worked, and popular opinion started to move in Sperlich's direction. Finally, the project code named T115 finally began.

In May 1983, on the cover of *Car and Driver* magazine, five members of the Detroit Pistons basketball team were pictured in front of a boxy little vehicle with a headline that read, "A Van for All Seasons." In the article the term *minivan*

> *IN THE ARTICLE THE TERM MINIVAN WAS COINED, AND A STAR WAS BORN.*

was coined, and a star was born. The article read, "Picture a van that is three inches shorter, ten inches narrower, and fifteen inches lower from the road to roof than the next smallest van on the market, yet has enough room for the Detroit Pistons and their luggage and can be stuffed into your garage just like a normal automobile."[47]

The success of the minivan came from a combination of ideas. Just as he had done years before at Ford, Sperlich had taken an existing and successful platform and put a new spin on it. The result in both cases was something new for which the market was ready. The Baby Boomers had grown older and had children of their own, and the minivan was the perfect car for their middle-aged needs.

The resulting Plymouth Voyager and Dodge Caravan sold like crazy. The competition was completely blindsided. Ford and General Motors had nothing close. All the other car companies scrambled to catch some of the success of these new vehicles, but the vans they made still drove like vans, sucked gas like vans, and felt like vans. Chrysler continued to make improvements while the others struggled. Toyota produced a minivan, but the engine was right between the two front seats, and the van sat too high, requiring customers to climb into it. Chrysler owned the market for nearly two decades!

Five months after the release of the Voyager and Caravan, Chrysler paid out the first dividends on its stock in five years. In August of that year, Chrysler announced it had paid back its loan from the government in full, and seven years early. It was a complete turnaround.

Ingrassia wrote, "Sperlich retired in 1988 with both the Mustang and the minivan on his resume. Either one would have been commendable, having orchestrated both was remarkable."[48] Iacocca and Sperlich weren't Baby Boomers but a little older. They nailed the needs of the largest generation in US history, though, first with the Mustang and then with the minivan.

The minivan became a symbol in our society of a certain demographic. The term "soccer mom" came into our vernacular, and the multitasking, minivan-driving super-women became a powerful political force. The image of a minivan with a stick figure family on the back heading off to the soccer game is just about the best encapsulation of American suburban life for middle-class families in the past twenty or thirty years. When a new product succeeds, that's something. But when a product becomes part of and helps shape a new subculture, then you really have something.

MINDSET MEMOS

1. Failure isn't fatal if it informs future decisions.
If you learn what caused the failure, then there really is no failure at all. Ford totally failed with the Edsel but realized they were not being responsive to what the market wanted. Having learned that lesson, they were able to tailor the Mustang to the right demographic at the right time.

Sperlich was fired from Ford, and that might have felt like a failure, but he was able to keep going and roll that experience into his next big win. Other people can't define you as a failure. Sperlich believed in his ideas and came out winning in the end.

2. Catching the trend isn't easy, but it has a huge payoff.
You need to zoom out and look at the bigger picture. Predicting the future is hard, but if you are aware, you can spot trends and work with them and not against them. Gain a broad perspective, and you will

get clues as to what is coming. It's easy to get lost in the minutiae of what you do on a daily basis and lose the big picture. Get the big picture, catch a trend or two, and it can pay very well.

3. Leverage what you've got to get what you want.

The Mustang was built on the Falcon platform, and the minivan was built on the K car platform. Build on your momentum, and run with your victories until you build them into something bigger and better.

4. Don't ride past success forever.

Sperlich and Iacocca could have basked in their Mustang success. That would have been enough, and they still would have been famous and considered automotive geniuses. They would have missed the second round at Chrysler, though, and their largest successes, their most significant impact.

Don't ever just rest on that one big success. There is always more out there for you to do.

5. Look for new combinations.

Steve Jobs described creativity as coming up with new combinations. For example, a new music act combines country and rap. This doesn't sound like the likeliest combination, but it's super popular.

Someone decided to make a bacon-vanilla shake. That sounds like it might be terrible, but it's actually good. Another food combination that has gotten popular is salt in chocolate. You wouldn't normally think that those would go together, but maybe someone spilled the salt into the chocolate in the kitchen by accident, and it turned out to be a thing. Sperlich's van/car combo was genius, and it represents a pattern of productive creativity through creative combinations.

6. Be open to what new technology could mean, not to what it can do.

There's a huge difference between these two. What matters isn't what technology can do but rather what it can *mean*. Front-wheel drive wasn't just a different way to power a car to Sperlich—it was a way to completely rethink the car. What it could do was important because of what it meant. It meant more room. It meant higher fuel economy. It meant thinking about what a car and a van are in an entirely different way. Be alert to what technology could mean. Don't worry so much about what it does.

7. Life is not fair.

Negative stuff happens. Sometimes you get cold-cocked right in the face, and you're fuzzy headed, barely standing on your feet, with blood dripping from your chin. Take your shots—then begin again, better. It's not fair, and there is nothing you could have done to avoid it. When life does that to you, it's a chance to clear your head, get a fresh look, and try again.

8. Never stop fighting for a good idea.

Sperlich spent fifteen to twenty years trying to get the minivan idea implemented. That is one of the longest gestational periods in industrial history. That's a lot of perseverance on the part of one visionary engineer. Model his example with your own tenacity.

9. Improve your methods of persuasion.

Sperlich went from badgering Henry Ford unsuccessfully, to writing a very effective piece of satire that brought people around in a productive way. The selling of your idea may just need a creative new approach.

10. Partnerships are powerful.

When you find someone with whom you can partner in a productive, long-term enterprise, it's amazing what even just two of you can accomplish, especially if leading a pack of others. Sperlich and Iacocca are one of the shining examples of a productive partnership over the course of decades at two different companies. What productive partnerships have you had in your life?

11. Not everyone will want your masterpiece.
Some people refuse to drive a minivan. Not everyone is going to love what you do, and the surest way to fail is to try to please everyone. Go out there and do what you do, for those you do it for, and do it with all your heart. You will impact the ones it's actually for, and you can forget the rest.

CHAPTER

9

PAINTER OF LIGHT

Balance, peace, and joy are the fruit of a successful life. It starts with recognizing your talents and finding ways to serve others by using them.

—THOMAS KINKADE

His father abandoned his family when Thomas was only six years old. He remembered looking out the window of their small mobile home, waiting for his mother to come home from one of her many jobs. He would watch to see if she had a bag of groceries under her arm, because if she did, that meant that they would have dinner that night. If she didn't, then they would have to skip dinner and go hungry. Thomas promised himself that when he grew up, he would never go hungry again.

Thankfully, Thomas had an escape from his sometimes difficult life: he could draw. In grade school he made realistic, funny caricatures of the teachers nobody liked and was actually able to sell them to other students. That was one of his first hints that art might be his ticket to a better life.

When Thomas was eleven, a local painter named Charles Bell took him on as an apprentice. At age sixteen, Thomas apprenticed to a more esteemed and accomplished artist, Glenn Wessels. Wessels and Ansel Adams, the famous "photographer of the world," were great friends. They had been in a Jeep accident together while on an adventure in the Sierras, and Wessels had been injured. He was quite frail and so needed a helper, and that was why he was willing to take on and teach an apprentice. The apprentice, in turn, would help compensate for his physical impairments.

Wessels was well placed in the art world. He had been trained at the Académie Colarossi in Paris. He had been appointed California Commissioner of Fine Arts, and he served on the boards of both the San Francisco Art Institute and the Oakland Museum. He had been friends with Ernest Hemingway, Pablo Picasso, and Gertrude Stein. Wessel thrilled young Thomas with stories of the art world and with advanced techniques of painting. Wessels instilled in Thomas what it meant to live the life of an artist, and Thomas began to believe in himself, to believe that he could make it in the art world.

Thomas went to study at the University of California at Berkeley and then to the Art Center of Design in Pasadena, where he delivered pizzas on his motorcycle to make a minimal living. At this time, Thomas became aware of the friction between staying true to his art, or the "artist's vision," and the need to actually earn a living. It's the classic "making a difference" versus "making a living" conflict. Thomas wanted to make beautiful art—it was his gift—but he also had to eat.

> THOMAS WANTED TO MAKE BEAUTIFUL ART—IT WAS HIS GIFT—BUT HE ALSO HAD TO EAT.

He had a good friend whom he had met at the art school. They did some thinking and dreaming together, and came up with a plan to quit school and pursue art full time. Their concept was that they would be a lot like hobos, riding trains and camping around a fire near the junkyards in the evenings. They would be free spirits, and they would be able to paint whenever and wherever and however they would like. Of course, this didn't last very long because they got hungry!

Somehow they landed a job painting landscape backdrops for movie sets and soundstages in Hollywood. Thomas painted more than seven hundred movie sets in all throughout those years. As he painted those landscapes, he realized he was good at adding imaginative elements. Instead of painting the landscapes as they really were, he would idealize them, stylize them, and bring them to life in a way that people appreciated. Author G. Eric Kuskey, a man who worked for Thomas for many years, wrote how Thomas was touched a little by Hollywood. He started calling himself the "painter of light." Thomas Kinkade had found his niche.

Thomas set himself up in a little cottage where he painted small landscape paintings, and he sold them in the parking lots of local grocery stores. In a humble way, he began living his dream life. His cottage was at the bend of a small road near a big red barn on a neighboring farm, not too far from where he was born. The cottage had log walls, a chimney that smoked from the natural fire in the fireplace, and wood frame windows looking out on the forest behind. The place was a lot like the scenes he would paint throughout his life.

This could have been the extent of the story for Thomas Kinkade. He was an artist scratching out his living doing art on his own terms. Many artists aren't so lucky. But Thomas had a driving ambition beyond that of most artists. Maybe it came from his upbringing and hunger in that little mobile home or from the abandonment by his father. Whatever the reason, he was driven to do more, and his art would eventually strike a chord with people all around the world.

One Saturday morning Thomas was at a little art fair in Carmel-by-the-Sea, California. He had his canvas set up and was displaying several of his landscapes. Advertising his wares this way was his norm, and he sold a few paint-ings here and there. A little crowd had gathered around to watch him work. A thirty-four-year-old Kirby vacuum cleaner salesman named Rick Barnett walked out of a cigar shop nearby and just happened to notice the crowd around this artist, who sat on a little stool, painting one of his landscapes. As Barnett drew closer, he was amazed by a couple of things. One was the ease with which Thomas painted and brought the colors to life so quickly. He also noticed how gregarious and engaging Thomas was as he interacted with the small audience. Thomas was just an average, everyday guy, full of personality, talking to these people in an easy manner, enjoying their company.

Barnett was a successful salesman who made great money. As he watched Thomas paint and interact with the crowd, the thought occurred to him that he could sell those paintings. When the crowd had dispersed, Barnett took the opportunity to approach Thomas and explain what he thought he could do for him. They traded business cards and agreed to stay in touch.

Next, Thomas met a man named Ken Raasch at a wedding reception. Ken had always dreamed of starting his own business. When it was time to leave the reception, they had agreed to go into business together.

The artist, the salesman, and the businessman formed a little triumvirate, and the enterprise was launched. Thomas's work, they thought, would have universal appeal, so they would reproduce the art for a larger audience. They produced a series of lithographs, or reproductions, to market. These reproductions were produced, serialized, numbered, and signed by the author for authenticity. A limited number of each was produced so that they would be valuable by being rare. This was not all that uncommon, but Thomas was still unknown. Because of Thomas's creativity and wide appeal, the three were certain they could sell these reproductions. Thomas's personality helped. Everyone loved him, and they leveraged his appeal as a person every chance they could to build the brand.

The three worked for more than three years, slowly building up the fan base for Thomas's work. Thomas was painting constantly, Ken labored to position his work in the marketplace and managed the production of the lithographs and framing, and Rick was out doing the selling.

They got their first break when the Bradford Exchange, a collectibles giant, saw Thomas's work at an art expo in New York and signed a deal to print the art on a huge array of memorabilia. Thomas's company would receive a 5 percent royalty on every item sold — coffee mugs, aprons, napkin holders, salt and pepper shakers, etc. — all with Kinkade's unique and interesting landscapes printed on them. This deal became a key source of income for the company in its early lean years. This also achieved the goal of getting exposure for the paintings and for Thomas and helped build the growing fan base.

This process also helped the company clarify its target demographic. The Bradford Exchange advertised in *Parade* magazine, with full-page ads on the back featuring items with Kinkade's landscapes printed on them. Kuskey writes about how they now really understood who would respond best to these paintings. The highbrow art collectors just weren't that interested. Kinkade's true demographic were the "steadfast, middle American, Christian ladies with Hummel figurines at home."[5]

Within two years, sales through the Bradford Exchange exceeded $20 million. At that point they were able to expand into the lucrative greeting card business. Every imaginable kind of collectible started appearing with Thomas Kinkade's artwork on it. They were able to sign all sorts of licensing agreements.

Thomas produced as many as fifteen major new works each year. Most of them required at least fifty layers of paint and took nearly three hundred hours to complete. He would work on several paintings at a time, moving from one to the other.

Demand exceeded supply, and they decided to create even better reproductions of the paintings. They created a canvas transfer system that would go beyond lithographed copies and result in a more valuable product. They made photographic prints from the original work and laid them in vats of glue in an atmosphere-controlled room. Then, once they were dry, they took these photographs of the paintings and bonded them to actual canvases, like those on which Thomas painted. Master highlighters then added more layers of paint and features that gave it the same look as the originals. Hundreds of highlighters worked at easels layering on paint to produce paintings as true to the originals as possible.

At first, Thomas signed each one of these, but there were quickly just too many to do, so they automated the signature with an ink stamp of his signature. To meet the requirements of authenticity, the ink for these stamps actually contained some of Thomas Kinkade's blood. Now each canvas transfer reproduction had the painter's DNA and could be authenticated without a doubt.

They sold these paintings by the thousands, and the canvas transfer reproductions now sold for significantly more. They printed them in more sizes and in more series with larger editions. At first these reproductions were sold in editions limited to twenty-five hundred prints, selling for an average of about $1,200 apiece. They soon began to expand the editions to ten thousand, with some getting as large as thirty thousand. The prices for these paintings began to rise, and demand was high.

They then started to license calendars, and they made a deal with Avon for the art to be on the cover of their catalog. All through this meteoric rise, Thomas continued to be the friendly, congenial face of the brand. He also continued to paint nonstop.

A born-again Christian, Thomas felt a deep purpose and calling behind his work. His reason for painting was that he wanted to "touch people with my painting." Kuskey comments, "His paintings became devotions to God and Jesus. He had a mission and a purpose for his life and his art."[51]

Thomas was a reader, and he also traveled quite a bit in order to get ideas for his paintings. One of the most inspirationally productive places he went to was the Cotswolds in England. It's a green, hilly place with quaint little cottages among the hills. Later, Kinkade would tell people that the Cotswolds was a place where he got some of the "secret sauce" behind his paintings.

He studied those warm, snuggly cottages, noticing what he liked about them and what things about them weren't quite right.

They would have a door a little bit smaller than a door should be or a window tucked right up into the gable where you shouldn't put a window. He noticed that those imperfections were what made the cottages so appealing and endearing. He began to include some of these concepts in his art. He had already mastered the effect of making the painting look as though it was alive with light, but now he added these little imperfections that would be just as endearing to people as the Cotswold cottages. It was his secret: "the charm of chaos."[52]

Kinkade knew he was a bit of a rebel in the art world. He went against the grain of the art purist by his "unholy" alliance between business and art. The critics also thought his art was formulaic and somewhat unoriginal. In addition, it was just too positive for the usual art connoisseur's taste. His combination of business, art, and driving ambition put him parallel with greats such as Walt Disney and Steve Jobs. Each in his own way combined elements of artistic genius with business skill. Kuskey wrote, "Thomas's success almost seemed to be mocking its veneration of the concept of the original art object by producing the canvas transfers and adding dollops

> "HIGH CULTURE IS PARANOID ABOUT SENTIMENT, BUT HUMAN BEINGS ARE INTENSELY SENTIMENTAL."
> —THOMAS KINKADE

of paint, thereby making a copy unique and original again. It almost became a postmodern exercise in the semiotics of art." Kinkade himself said, "High culture is paranoid about sentiment, but human beings are intensely sentimental."[53]

Kinkade realized who his true customer was. It wasn't the snooty, overeducated person who understood a certain type of art from an intellectual perspective; it was the person who just enjoyed art for the honest feeling it invoked in the viewer, and he continued to paint for that true customer alone. He didn't worry about what the critics said or what the supposed experts would say. Thomas called himself "the Trojan horse in the enemy camp."[54]

Kinkade and his company had hit on an interesting and powerful combination. For one thing, people get attached to products produced in a series. Like a John Grisham novel, Thomas's paintings were eagerly awaited by thousands of fans who just couldn't wait for the next one. The other part of the combination is that people like the exclusivity of owning an original. In the art world, original paintings can become very valuable. Thomas and his partners figured out a way to have both elements working for them, and they were able to do it on a large scale. It was not only a creative combination, it was a very profitable one as well.

Sales for the company continued to skyrocket. New and more lucrative licensing deals were struck. A subdivision in California was named after Kinkade's work and dedicated to resembling the buildings in his paintings. He was even involved with the architects, determining what the facades of some of these homes would look like, as well as helping design some of the community features. A Thomas Kinkade furniture line was launched and was hugely successful.

The company began selling franchises of Thomas Kinkade Gallery stores that would open in towns and malls to display and sell his work. These stores had warm fireplaces and comfortable rocking chairs to create an environment similar to what you felt when looking at one of his paintings. It was as if one of the paintings had come to life, and you were able to enter one of those quaint cottages. Thomas released his new paintings at these stores, giving a speech and unveiling the new work. The stores were a great success, at first.

The Thomas Kinkade Company went public, and its shares began to be traded on the stock market—the first ever artist to be publicly traded on a stock exchange. By the time Thomas died in 2012, sales of his art had brought in more than $4 billion.

As the money rolled in, some problems began to arise. There was infighting among the executives of the company. Things got turbulent. At one point, the company, due to mismanagement, declared bankruptcy and laid off more than one-third of its workforce. Some of the original people in the company were forced out.

Under the pressures of meeting the short-term quarterly report expectations of investors in the public stock, the sales arm began to control the direction of the company. They brought people in who believed in high-pressure sales, and there was simply more pressure to move more paintings. They ended up overselling the galleries to the franchisees, and the locations were too close to each other, competing for the same market. They forced the franchise galleries to buy a certain amount of art on a schedule and dictated the prices at which the galleries had to sell the art. At the same time, the company began selling the same art available at the galleries on QVC but at a discount. The company further undercut their franchisees by making a deal with discount retailer Tuesday Morning to sell the paintings for even less than they were charging on QVC. A painting you could have bought at one of the beautiful, cozy galleries for $390 you could now buy for $59 from Tuesday Morning.

The predictable result was that the galleries started failing, and a large group of franchise owners banded together and sued the company. The greedy drive for more sales at the cost of integrity ruined the brand. Thomas Kinkade himself was conflict averse and let things go the wrong way for too long. He used most of his own money to buy back enough stock to pull the company off of the public exchanges and go private again. By that time the brand had suffered irreparable damage.

All this pressure through these turbulent years led to the worsening of Thomas's drinking problem, to the point where his wife and daughters staged an intervention. Thomas never forgave his wife for this, and it marked the end of his marriage of thirty-plus years. He only warmed up to his daughters again slowly. As with many artists, Thomas's personal life was a mess by the time he died, only fifty-four years old, from a combination of alcohol poisoning and Valium. Almost as in a script from a bad Hollywood movie, there was an opportunistic mistress causing a scene over the estate.

Kuskey wrote,

Thomas was really no different than any great artist you read about in the history books. They were all tortured, driven by demons, and haunted by vices that often took them too young. Thomas was sensitive. He was obsessed, and had no choice in life but to paint. Art was his lifeline and his destruction. Perhaps a certain amount of suffering is necessary for any artist to be great. It's the question of what comes first, which might never be answered: Are you an artist because you suffer, or do you suffer because you're an artist?[55]

Whether or not that's true, it seems there were three big errors in his life that brought on his troubles.

The first was taking the company public. The move was a strategic error. Art doesn't thrive under the intense pressure of meeting quarterly earnings report expectations.

The pressure to sell the art led to short-term thinking and tragic diminishing of the brand.

The second problem was Thomas's hands-off attitude toward his own company. They used his name, his art, his images, and literally his blood, and while he was busy in his own world painting and producing the fuel that was consumed by this ever-growing fire, company management tainted his image and ruined his name. His ostrich approach to conflict and problems was a major part of his downfall.

The third and most damaging problem was alcoholism. Private demons can be an all-consuming fire that should never be underestimated or ignored.

Even though the story ended tragically, there are many positive applications that we can take from his life. That an artist sold over $4 billion of his art in such a short time, and while he was still alive, is unheard of. There was a lot right about the way Kinkade led his life. He sought to make the world better through the gift God had given him, and he returned the glory to that Creator who had given him those talents.

MINDSET MEMOS

1. Early struggles can create the hunger for high achievement.

How often do we read about someone who achieves amazing things in her career, but in her life story, everything was just perfect? That hardly ever seems to happen. Usually she had to work through some kind of trouble, deprivation, or struggle. We don't want those hard things to happen (to us or to our children), but the hunger for truly great achievement seems to come about when a person has it tough for a while.

This is not to say you should strive for anything less than a wonderful, prosperous, loving home for your family. For those who have it hard and learn to use that hunger in the right way, however, it may even be an advantage.

2. Mentors and the right training are important.

No matter how much talent we are endowed with naturally, we need to put in the hours and develop that talent. We need mentors to show us how to hone that raw talent into a refined skill.

The Beatles played in Germany every single night for hours upon hours, honing and perfecting their natural skill before they made it big and came to the United States. Those thousands of hours of playing gave them confidence and proficiency that they might not have had otherwise.

Kinkade was painting from the moment he could as a young child. He apprenticed at the age of eleven and then at sixteen. He worked in the movie industry, painting hundreds of backdrops in a short time. This allowed him to develop and fine-tune his craft and helped him to hone in on what made him special as an artist.

3. Striving for purpose and meaning doesn't have to mean you don't make money.

If you are going to pursue what you love, you don't have to take a vow of poverty. If you go after money only, you will never find fulfillment there. You can, however, put money and meaning together. Many people have.

To do so, you have got to find out what you've really got—what your talents really are. What are your gifts? What has God given you? What do you have that is special? When you find the answers, put in the time and discover ways to serve others with those gifts. Then you are on your way to true prosperity.

4. Sometimes, you have to make risky moves in your life.

Risk is an interesting word because it means different things to different people. Some think risk is when you veer off the path of what people expect you to do: go to school, work hard, get your degrees, get a good job, keep your nose clean, work your way up, and make sure you hold down your good-paying job that has good benefits and a good retirement plan.

Maybe that whole plan is more risky than finding and following your true calling. Maybe playing it safe is the most dangerous thing you can do in our world. What if *safe* is the new *risky*?

Thomas and his college friend left the traditional path to go risk it on their own. That might have not worked out in the short term, but in the long term it led Thomas to the Hollywood job and then to greatness.

There is a big difference between risky and reckless. When you make a gutsy decision—a bold move that's aligned with your principles, dreams, and highest calling—it's not risky at all. When you live your life the way everybody else tells you to, follow someone else's program that isn't true to your calling in life—*that's* reckless.

5. It takes time to scale up.

Art is one of the most solitary activities you could ever do. Thomas Kinkade didn't need help making his masterpieces. No one else showed up at that easel to paint any portion of those original works. He labored away by himself in that little cottage, producing those paintings at a clip of fifteen a year, three hundred hours each, every one involving fifty layers of paint.

Kinkade was successful on a large scale, though, because he assembled a team. He found talented, ambitious people with whom he clicked. They formed a mastermind, feeding off one another's creativity and mutually complementing their talents. This team allowed a simple artist's singular work to scale up until it became an enormous enterprise that boggles the imagination. It took time, and it took teamwork, but ultimately they took it big.

6. Discover who your real customer is.

Find out why your customers love you and why you appeal to them, and keep doing it. Kinkade knew exactly what resonated with people, and he kept giving them what they wanted. He knew why his art worked for his audience.

7. Innovate and grow.

The canvas transfer process they came up with might have been unusual, but it was ingeniously innovative. The process allowed them to meet the customer demand for everybody who wanted to hang one of these works of art above their fireplace. No one had thought of using that kind of process before, and it allowed the business to grow.

8. Go against the grain, and create new combinations.

Business blended with art. Selling a series along with the exclusivity of owning an original. These ideas clash and compete, but when Kinkade and his team found a way to do both, it was a key to their success.

Don't be afraid to offend the status quo. It's the job description of a leader to do so. If someone isn't whining that you're not doing it right, then you are probably not leading. You certainly aren't innovating. If you want a nice, cozy little life, don't threaten the status quo. If you want an exciting, exhilarating, wild ride, threaten the status quo, and see what happens. It won't bring peace, but it will bring entertainment.

9. Guard your brand.

As the Kinkade team recognized early on, you are your own brand. How you show yourself to the world, what unique value you bring, and your contribution—together, they all constitute a brand.

You need to guard and protect it. Never let short-term considerations or pressures undermine your long-term legacy. You only have one you.

10. Finish well.

Stay focused on the big picture, and guard against personal demons. Everybody is attacked and tempted. Everybody has weaknesses. Don't take those things lightly. If someone as talented, good-hearted, and warm-spirited as Thomas Kinkade can be brought down the way he was, then what does that say about the rest of us? His life and his tragic end should serve as a great warning to us that, if we want to do great things and glorify our God, it won't be without opposition. We need to be on guard. We need to finish well.

LEADERSHIP BY DESIGN

Being superficially different is the goal of so many of the products we see ... rather than trying to innovate and genuinely taking the time, investing the resources and caring enough to try and make something better.

—JONY IVE

*T*here's a reason Apple computer fans are so loyal—the products are that user-friendly and intuitive. Steve Jobs was the genius people saw as the face of Apple. Jobs didn't work alone, though. He worked with other geniuses to produce these innovative products. One of them was Jony Ive.

Jony was born in Chingford, England. His father was an expert in industrial design, and he fostered an engagement with design throughout Jony's childhood. At that time England and Wales happened to become the first two countries in the world to make design technology education available to all children between the ages of five and sixteen in their public school systems. Jony plugged into this program and thrived in it, learning from his father as well.

Jony learned the key elements of the creative process. First was drawing and sketching. In the design world, these skills are what you would call the craft side of design. You draw and sketch to come up with ideas. The other side of design is the communication side. That is when you talk things through and discuss them with others. In every endeavor, those two need to be there hand in hand in order for you to be successful. You have to have both the craft and the communication.

Ive was a stellar student and could have gotten into Oxford or Cambridge as he came out of high school. Instead, he chose to attend Newcastle Polytechnic, which later changed its name to Northumbria University. It's still regarded as the top school in the United Kingdom for industrial design. By the time he started there, he had already won one of the most prestigious design awards in England.

He quickly developed his own design style and language. Ive had a clean, minimalist style to his designs. His memory of the time, though, was that the experience was less than ideal. "In some ways I had a pretty miserable time. I did nothing other than work."[57]

Ive was gifted and humble, however, and was sponsored by one of the world's preeminent design companies, Roberts Weaver Group in London, or RWG. There, Jony met a senior designer named Clive Grinyer, who said of

Jony, "Most design students have lots of ego and very little talent. Jony was the other way around."[58]

While still a student, Jony designed a special kind of pen, which actually went into production as a real product. Students at design school hardly ever get their designs produced. According to Grinyer, Ive's designs were incredibly simple and elegant. They were usually surprising but then made complete sense once you understood them.

Jony had a penchant for "finishing" — putting the final touches to his designs that would take them from good to great. David Tonge, a fellow student at the time, said, "The level of finish was what was always amazing about his work relative to others. Others were and are capable of the conceptual thought and creativity, but very few are capable of that level of finish. It's still the standout component of his work."[59]

Jony was also a hard worker. He was prolific. When other students built up a handful of models to test a design concept, Jony Ive would make a hundred of them. He would do ten times the modeling and testing the average design student did. Building scores of models and prototypes would later become his trademark at Apple.

He was interested in the hardware *and* software side of products. He was interested in their interface. It's as if Jony was custom-made for his later endeavors.

Ive was shown a Mac computer for the first time in college, and he loved it. He said, "It unapologetically pointed to an alternative in a complacent and creatively bankrupt industry. Apple stood for something and had a reason for being that wasn't just about making money."[60] He was drawn to the design of the product, and he knew there had to be a story behind that design. As a design prodigy himself, he understood what it meant and what it took for a company to produce a product like that. He appreciated the minimalist design, the easy user interface, and the innovation of housing it all in one box. He made note of Apple computer as a company to keep tabs on.

Ive didn't go to work at Apple right after college, though. He joined a top London design firm and then struck out with others from there to form a start-up design firm. Jony became one of the top names in design. He did some consulting work for Apple as part of that start-up, and Apple finally recruited him in 1992. He moved his family from London to California and settled into a job at the Apple design studio.

Unfortunately, this was during the time when Steve Jobs was absent from Apple. Jobs had been more or less booted from his own company, and Apple went from being an exciting, creative, technology- and design-driven company to a bloated, bureaucratic mess without any sense of direction.

Despite a research and development budget above $200 million, Apple's design studio had no disciplined product pipeline and no coordination between the groups involved. It was no longer the company that had conceived of the elegant Mac design that had originally caught Ive's attention. As a result, he hadn't been there long before he became disillusioned. He considered leaving and not for the last time. He was talked into staying, though, and he agreed to stick it out to see what might happen.

Bob Brunner was the designer who had recruited Jony, and he was in charge of the design group at Apple. Bob instituted a structure that would end up paying large dividends for the company. He separated Apple's designers into a stand-alone group. He gave them their own space and closed it off from the rest of the company. He didn't install cubicles but created an open space, with everybody's desks in the same large room. The designers could dress as informally for work as they liked. Because they shared this space, they were more or less forced to collaborate. They had brainstorming meetings at least twice a week in what they called their kitchen. Food was brought in, and these great design minds would sit around and kick ideas back and forth.

Brunner created a culture, with its loose structure, collaborative workflow, and consultancy mindset, which was basically its own thing apart from the bureaucratic and stagnant feel of the rest of the company. As such, they had to sink or swim based upon the quality of their design. It was as if they were their own consultancy, instead of being a part of a large company. This resulted in a small, tight, cohesive group of extremely talented designers working on challenges together and coming up with great stuff.

Brunner did one more thing that ended up paying huge dividends in the future. He left the company, but as he did, he made the choice of naming the twenty-nine-year-old Ive as his successor. The move was controversial. They could have hired a more experienced person or done a wide, expensive search to bring in talent, but Brunner knew he had the right guy already on the team. Brunner said of Ive, "He has the full-spectrum mentality. He loves the big picture, but he revels in the details. It was probably one of the better recommendations I ever made."[61] That was an obvious understatement. Brunner built a great studio, hired great talent, set up a culture, and then left Jony Ive in charge of it. It was quite the virtuoso performance.

But Apple was tanking and fast. Microsoft's Windows 95 had ripped off almost all of Mac's user interface features. Apple's market share plummeted to less than 3 percent. The CEO position of the company became a revolving door. Internally, the company was fractured and split into dozens of little fiefdoms. It had become consensus driven. In a knee-jerk reaction to the top-down way that Jobs had run the company, Apple had adopted the touchy-feely attitude that everyone had to agree before a decision was made.

Apple was getting clobbered and not able to deal with it well because decisions were not being made efficiently. Bureaucratic interference kept designs from getting approved, and they couldn't get funding for new ideas. Ive had had enough, and he thought seriously again about leaving. But he was talked into staying yet again, this time by the new head of the hardware department, who oversaw the design department as well. Jony was given a raise and told to hang on; things would get better. This couldn't have been more right.

After a twelve-year hiatus, Jobs was brought back to Apple, which acquired the education computer company Jobs had started when he left. The new company hadn't done well, but Apple needed the software Jobs's team had developed for what he called his workstation computers. So Steve was back, and it wasn't long before he was again calling the shots.

Jony Ive said of his new boss, "I remember very clearly Steve announcing that our goal is not just to make money, but to make great products."[62] This was a counterintuitive statement, given the state Apple was in at the time. The company was bleeding millions of dollars a week and needed money fast. It would be logical to focus on where you could make money most quickly, like selling current inventory or cutting costs. Jobs was sure that instead the way forward was to make awesome products, and that was what they set about to do.

To do it, Jobs advocated a design ethic. He believed the company would live or die based on whether it was a company that designed marvelous products and made design the center of everything they produced. Little could Jobs have known how well equipped the Apple design studio was for this challenge. Given the studio Brunner had built and the genius of Jony Ive leading it, they were poised to make history.

Consider the iPhone as the example of this design team in action. Jony's team had gathered for their twice-a-week brainstorming meeting in the kitchen. In this meeting you could put anything on the table. What had made the Macintosh successful was the user interface. It was the mouse and ease of input and control. Someone at this meeting had the audacity to ask, "How do we get rid of the mouse and keyboard entirely?" They brainstormed on how someone could interact with a computer in ways other than a traditional keyboard and mouse. That is a very disruptive and revolutionary question to ask if you are working for the company whose products pioneered such features.

One of the engineers at this brainstorming meeting had been working on multi-touch pads. These were the pads commonly used on laptops, a little square that you drag your finger across to control the cursor. Another engineering group at Apple had been working on this technology and had discovered some amazing things. What if they built the multi-touch pad right into the screen? With that impetus, they built the first iPhone. It was as big as a ping-pong table. They projected images down onto it, and found you could move your fingers to scroll, twist them to rotate. No one had done that before. You could pinch and widen your fingers to control the size of an image. All this seems inevitable today, but it was revolutionary. When Ive saw this, he said, "This is going to change everything."[63] He wanted to show Jobs, but he had to wait and do it in the right way.

If you have read about Steve Jobs, you know he shot from the hip, intuitively. He had extremely good instincts, and he trusted those instincts. Also, you know he didn't suffer fools lightly, to be polite about it. He had the reputation of making decisions in public, and you didn't want to be on the wrong end of those decisions. Ive knew he had to stage-manage this for his boss. The thing ran on simulated software and wasn't ready for prime time.

Ive's usual approach was to have his guys make up several different models of what they wanted to do, and they'd put all the crappy ones first. Jobs would dismiss the crap, and then when they brought out the good one, it would look so good by comparison that Jobs would have to consider it. In this case, Ive made sure Jobs was shown this new idea in private. Immediately, Jobs knew this was the future. This was the direction they were going to go. Another company was developing the multi-touch technology, and Apple quietly bought it and took all that company's products off the market. They knew they had something big.

In 2005, over 40 million iPods were sold. It was obvious to Apple that sooner or later someone would combine an iPod-type device with a phone, but Apple wanted to be first. To begin, they simply threw a phone function on the iPod. One would dial the desired phone numbers with the control wheel. This was not great, especially when you consider what they finally brought out.

They decided to go wholeheartedly into the mobile phone market. They had no credibility in that area. The phone industry was dominated by giants. It was an enormous undertaking with considerable risk. Apple's attorney said, "Had the project gone wrong, it could have destroyed the company."[64]

They began the project in secret, of course, and locked it down even tighter than normal. They tried several designs, including the multi-touch one, but couldn't get it to work. According to author Leander Kahney, "It was fundamental R&D in all directions. It meant ramping up probably the most difficult project in a company's history and all the while continuing to develop product, like the MacBook and the iPod line." That's the problem with being an innovator. You have to destroy what you have so you can build it better for the future, while still building and maintaining what you are working on in the present. They had some big winners on their hands, but they didn't just rest there. They disrupted their own success story with even more new and promising innovation. Very few companies are able to do that.

At one point they had to scrap all their designs and back up. In a gutsy move, they decided to try glass for the screen of the iPhone. No one had ever done glass in a portable device. Jobs said, "I won't sell a product that gets scratched. I want a glass screen and I want it perfect in six weeks."[65] The glass they found that worked was a thirty-five-year-old technology. They discovered that Corning had created a nearly unbreakable glass they called "muscle glass." The trade name for the product was ChemCORE, and it had never taken off. It had been discontinued in 1971. They hadn't made it in thirty-four years. Jobs contacted Corning and told them that he would buy whatever they could make, as much as possible.

Corning's CEO told Jobs, "None of our plants make ChemCORE now." Can you imagine someone coming to you and wanting a product that you made thirty-four years ago? Jobs answered, "Get your mind around it. You can do it."[66] I guess if you're Steve Jobs, that's how you solve problems. You simply tell people they can meet an impossible expectation. And they did! Corning renamed it Gorilla Glass and found some factories that could make it quickly.

> YOU SIMPLY TELL PEOPLE THEY CAN MEET AN IMPOSSIBLE EXPECTATION. AND THEY DID!

By the fall of 2006 the iPhones prototypes were still a disaster. They flat-out wouldn't work. Apple had scheduled the rollout of the iPhone at Mac World in early 2007, and here in late 2006 it still didn't work. It dropped calls, and the apps got interrupted and stopped working, closing with no warning. A great example of the difficulties they faced was with the feature that turns the screen off when you put it to your ear so you don't accidentally press buttons with your face. That worked pretty well in testing unless you had long, dark hair. For some reason, if you were a long-haired brunette, it just didn't like you. The phone wouldn't get the message that it was being used as a phone, and your face would open apps, change the volume, and hang up, and no one could figure out why!

Kahney comments, "The problem was that everything was new and nothing worked."[67]

At one point, Jony Ive told Jobs, "We don't have a product."[68] This was weeks before it was to be announced at Mac World. Corning was making miles of glass for this device, the expectations were high, and Ive was saying that the product was not functional.

Kahney wrote that the iPod had been regarded by a lot of the tech world as Apple getting lucky—a fluke. When Apple entered the cutthroat cell phone world, many predicted the iPhone would flop. Microsoft's Steve Balmer predicted that it wouldn't get any market share.

Of course, it did. Jobs *did* roll out the iPhone at Mac World in 2007, and the Apple sold 3.7 million of them that first year. The success of the iPhone was an absolute grand-slam home run. It achieved numbers and market share no other company has yet touched. The iPhone revolutionized mobile phone technology and spawned many copycats and me-toos. It also inspired some companies to improve on the tech and a lot of innovation. The iPhone, though, was the original. It was all made possible by a herculean effort on the part of Jony Ive and his design team to solve a seemingly endless list of design challenges that few thought could be solved. It's one of the most dramatic, successful design achievements in technology history.

MINDSET MEMOS

1. Invest in mentoring and building people.

From the start, Ive was able to take advantage of mentors and training. His father taught him, the school system taught him, and he had many other mentors and people in his life as he went along who taught and encouraged him. Bob Brunner was one of those mentors who invested in Ive, and it paid off for Apple and for the world in a big way.

2. When you see something extraordinary, it's that way by design.

Nothing that is truly extraordinary came about by way of an accident. It was intentionally made that way.

3. Grand achievements are usually the result of both teamwork and spectacular leadership.

Success is never just the story of one leader. There are always stories behind the stories of those who work to help the leader—those who work as an important part of the team. You may be the leader in your home, at church, or on the job. Other places you're not the leader. You can't be the leader everywhere. Maybe you are on the team in your business, or you are one of several on the deacon board at church. There needs to be both leadership and teamwork to make a difference. A leader is nothing without a good team, and a team will flounder unless someone steps up to lead.

4. You must not only know your craft; you must be able to communicate it well also.
It's not enough to be competent technically. You have to also get competent relationally. Sometimes you can compensate for one by being really good in the other, but you really need to have both.

5. One of the most successful combinations is to be gifted and humble at the same time.
Ive has the ability to stay away from the spotlight. You maybe hadn't heard of him until you read this chapter. Ive is the most successful industrial designer in history, yet he does not self-aggrandize. He seems most concerned about putting a fantastic product on the market and into your hands. He makes ridiculous money and has a large ownership stake in Apple Computer, but these things don't drive him. His whole focus is on the excellence of design and the

products. He does what he does because that is what he does.

6. Build something marvelous, and don't worry about the money.
Be excellent, do something amazing, and the money will find you.

7. Have a penchant for finishing.
Put the finish on the finish. Most people will just kind of pencil-whip something and get it partway done. Ive's father told him, "If there's a job worth doing, it's worth doing right." Ive grew to love it when things are done in an excellent way, all the way to completion. Very few people are wired like that. Others may call that being nitpicky or a neat freak, but it's actually excellence when applied the right way.

Jony Ive said, "The decisive factor is fanatical care beyond the obvious stuff, the obsessive attention to details that are often overlooked."[69] When you go the extra mile to make what you do well become great, you won't have any legitimate competition.

8. Intentionally build the right culture, and then get the sharpest minds you can find for that culture.
If you can build a winning culture the way Bob Brunner did at Apple, then you can attract the best minds in the world in that category. It becomes a

self-fulfilling virtuous cycle, because who wouldn't want to work in that environment? People want to play on the winning team.

9. Form great partnerships.

Neither Steve Jobs nor Jony Ive accomplished what they did by themselves. Kahney writes, "A blending of epiphany thinking and practical implementation became the single characteristic of the Jobs/Jony collaboration."[70] The two of them working together created way more than one plus one equaling two.

10. Developments that seem inevitable now were not always that way.

We look back now and it seems inevitable. Of course someone was going to combine the ideas behind the mobile phone and iPod. Apple did it, and with style, but they could have failed. It wasn't inevitable. It could have happened in a much less effective way, much later, done by someone else.

How did Lincoln know to stick with Grant when he was being accused of being a drunkard? How did Grant know he should send Sherman to burn Richmond and Atlanta? There was nothing inevitable about the outcome of the Civil War or any war for that matter. We read history backwards and take it for granted that it turned out as it did. Look at the leaders, and ask yourself how they knew what to do when they helped things go the right way. You will gain useful insights into your own endeavors if you do.

11. Innovation is rarely a single big idea. Usually, a series of ideas are brought together in a new and better way.
In the case of the iPhone, part of the technology had come from the sixties. The glass technology had been created thirty-five years earlier. No one had combined the tech in the way Jony Ive and the design team at Apple had. The breakthrough consisted of tiny cumulative innovations, not one big sudden leap.

12. Foster the mindset that problems can be solved.
Many times when we are hit with challenges and roadblocks, we tend to get stuck. Remember that problems can be solved. Addictions can be overcome. Insurmountable obstacles *can* be surmounted. Mindset will make the difference. No matter what happens, just set the understanding that obstacles can and will be overcome. Jobs and Ive displayed that mindset.

13. "The real risk is to think it's safe to play it safe."[71]
That's what Jony Ive said and believed. It's one of the big reasons for the impact he made.

CARMEGGEDON LEADERSHIP

Don't believe your own press and don't give speeches. Corporate leadership has degenerated into personal aggrandizement.

—SERGIO MARCHIONNE

Sergio Marchionne was born in 1952 in Chieti, Italy. His father was a military policeman during World War II, and his mom was a survivor of the ethnic cleansing of her Croatian village. They married soon after the war, worked hard, and saved their money toward a house. The government decided to devalue the currency in order to fight inflation in 1947. Sergio's parents' savings went from enough to buy a house to barely enough to buy a pair of shoes for each of them.

Marchionne recalls this as one of his first memories: "I still remember the look of resilience on my mother's face when my parents told me that story. She said, 'You deal with it, and you move on.'" Sergio inherited his parents' ability to take hardship in stride. He was drilled in the value of discipline and hard work.

Education became a top priority for him.

His great mathematical ability was noticed by an elementary teacher while he was still very young. She encouraged his parents to get him as good an education as possible. Because there was not much opportunity in Italy at the time, his mother decided they should move to Canada. She had a sister there who was doing well, so Sergio and his family moved to Canada when he was fourteen.

He didn't speak any English. He was amazed by the extra-large American cars and that anyone would eat Foot Loops for breakfast. He didn't like school, and quit at age sixteen, though he was later forced to finish at a private school. By the age of eighteen, he was already the manager of the local branch of a major bank.

Banking came to him quickly, but he was not as good at being a manager. He said he gained two lasting lessons from that experience. One was that authoritative leadership worked, but came at too high a price. The other was he realized how far behind he'd fallen by being a rebel, dropping out of school, and getting the first job he could.

His older sister had gone on to become a college professor at the University of Toronto. She had written books and had both a radio and TV show. He felt overshadowed. Sergio decided he wanted to learn and developed a passion for studying. He went on to get degrees in philosophy, law, and business. Not bad for a high school dropout.

He was back to work again at age thirty-one, this time as an accountant. He happened to be involved in the boom in leveraged buyouts (LBOs). On the margin, companies would merge or take over other companies to grow larger. He was made a comptroller for one of the big mergers, in charge of all the other accountants — his first real position of leadership since the early bank experience.

Before long, he was made director of corporate development, and he came to realize he was talented in the area of finance. He had always been good with numbers. That experience led him to aspire to be a chief financial officer, so he quit his job and went to law school.

After earning his fourth degree, he was hired on as a vice president and then president of finance at one company. Then he switched companies and realized his ambition to become the chief financial officer.

Sergio still wasn't great with people at this point, but he did have one great trait others noticed: he had great negotiating skills. It was said of him that he was able to empathize with the person on the other side of the table and see things from the perspective of others. He was able to create win–win situations and help the different interests and sides come together on deals.

When his company was bought out and his job eliminated, he was noticed for his talent and taken on in the new company. They said of him, "Marchionne was not only a crack negotiator, but someone who could out-lawyer the lawyers and tear through balance sheets like they were Twinkies."[73]

Sergio and his young family then transferred to Switzerland, where he was named CFO by the end of the year and then CEO of that same company. He was forty-four years old. Whether or not people need to get four degrees, it is clear Sergio used his education to his great advantage. He had learned his craft.

Sergio was good at hitting financial targets, he was a great communicator, he had great strategic skills, and his financial skills were unquestioned. Investors loved him. He still had some issues when it came to leading. He was called impatient, and he had a temper. Subordinates found him hard to work for. He was called a "control freak," and they said he didn't take criticism well.

Excellence always polarizes. One of the quickest ways to accomplish nothing and remain mediocre is to try to please everyone. Leaders have to figure out what's right, become convinced, and then stand on those convictions. You can be kind and have people skills, you can care and empathize, but you have to stand firm on what you believe.

The company Marchionne now led had engineered a big three-way merger of companies in Switzerland. Marchionne drove all the negotiations. These heavy industry companies had the advantage of his expertise, and he orchestrated the whole thing to everyone's benefit. He made it happen.

When it came time to name the CEO of the new giant company, he was passed up. There never does seem to be a straight path to success. You can perform your work perfectly and do all the right things, but sometimes it doesn't go down the way you expect or want it to.

Sergio was disappointed, but he didn't panic. Umberto Agnelli, a member of the family that has controlled Fiat for almost a century, recognized Sergio's talent, and he offered Marchionne a job as CEO of a company called SGS, a Swiss-based provider of goods certification inspection services. SGS was one little company in the Fiat empire.

This is where the story gets interesting. Fiat was in trouble. The whole company was in a massive free fall. It was in so much chaos that it went through five CEOs in two years' time. Sergio ended up being the fifth.

As CEO, Sergio's philosophy was to get the right people on the bus, and get the wrong people off the bus. His overall goal was to implement a flat organizational structure. Fiat was the opposite of that, with bureaucracy built in.

When Marchionne took over Fiat, the first thing he did was clean out many of these unnecessary layers. He showed up to offices unannounced and interviewed people, asking what their role was with the company. Anybody who wasn't a leader or a risk-taker he let go, and he put the risk-takers in charge. One person who worked there at the time said, "What happened in 2004 was Marchionne got rid of at least a couple of layers in the organization over-night. He got rid of the people who already lost the game in their own minds and gave freedom to a bunch of young managers who had nothing to lose. Having nothing to lose gives you tremendous energy."[74]

He formed something called the Group Executive Council to get all the decision-makers in one room at one time. They would hear all the information, make a decision, and move on. Then, a week later, they would meet to do it again. Decision-making became fast and deliberate.

"It was really the creation of the GEC that did it," said one of the members, "He killed all the committees. It ended the bureaucracy. The GEC met regularly and decided all the investments then and there."[75]

> *IF YOU WANT TO EFFECT CHANGE, YOU'VE GOT TO WORK AT THE CULTURAL LEVEL.*

Marchionne quickly turned the culture around at Fiat. He understood that if you want to effect change, you've got to work at the cultural level. It's the same thing we need to do in our homes and our businesses. We must create a positive and productive culture if we want great things to happen.

Even then, Marchionne and his twenty-four-member GEC were up against long odds. Fiat was on the ropes. On January 13, 2003, *Fortune* magazine ran a cover with an upside-down Fiat which said, "Arrivederci, Fiat," which means, "Good-bye, Fiat." The article said, "Losses are mounting, workers are up in arms. The board is in revolt. Will Fiat exit the car business?" When your troubles make it onto the cover of an international magazine, you know you are up against tough odds.

Marchionne held that magazine up in front of his people and said, "This cover illustrates our situation today. I totally believe we have a chance to relaunch the company. If you follow me, you will see that within three years we will see the same magazine with the 500 right side up."[76] Sergio set forth a vision for his company. He created this imagery in their minds, anchoring them to victory. It is likely the Fiat employees were jaded by now, thinking this new CEO would be gone soon, just like the others. Still, they also must have sensed there was something different about Marchionne. He was a leader; the others were just managers.

Leadership isn't stacking up a group of people around you with the best credentials; leadership is about assembling a team of leaders. Leaders assemble leaders who will be a positive force in the culture and will work well with other leaders.

It takes a special kind of leader to do that because it's not comfortable. These leaders you assemble ask tough questions, buck the system, and don't kiss your ring in the morning when they walk in. When you come up with an idea, they don't nod and say yes just because you're the big boss. When you lead leaders, you get all sorts of push-back and honest and even brutal observations. You have to be tough and want results enough to put up with it all.

Marchionne had three objectives. Fiat needed new cars badly. All their cars were poorly designed, created no passion, and just weren't attractive to the market-place. In the car business, product that doesn't move is a huge problem. Costs stack up as those cars don't sell. Inventories build up. Do you cut your losses and sell them cheap? Do you keep the factories running to produce more cars that aren't selling? They had to come out with some new products fast. His second objective was to get an effective advertising campaign running for those new products, and that led to the third: he had to do this all without spending much money, since they didn't have much to spend.

The employees started to buy into Marchionne's vision. They looked back fondly after the whole thing turned out to be a success. Author Jennifer Clark wrote, "Long hours and the occasional bout of verbal abuse do not seem to cancel the sheer thrill of the corporate reinvention these groups unleashed under Marchionne's leadership."[77]

His ability to make snap strategic decisions on the back of presentations by his management team quickly won them over. "We were ready to go to our death following him," recalled a former brand manager. Sergio wasn't winning Mr. Congeniality awards, but he was making progress. He was kicking butt and taking names.

Clark writes, "Most groups have a potential for greatness that never quite takes off, but every so often the right person comes along that can put together a handful of superb people, set an impossible goal, engage them in a holy war, and let them rip."[78]

It happened at Disney when the company created the first-ever animated feature film, it happened at Apple, it happened with the Manhattan Project, at Xerox, and at the Palo Alto Research Center, and it happened at Fiat in 2004.

According to Clark, "Marchionne's team quickly realized their boss prized debate and conflicting views as good for business and wanting meetings to continue until a decision had been reached. One manager proudly reported in a meeting that his division had gone from losing 180 million euros a month to just 120 million euros, and Marchionne, at the end of his presentation, looked at him and said, 'We don't want anyone around here who's excited about losing. We want people who are on fire about winning. You are free to go.'"[79] He fired him on the spot.

After seventeen quarters of losses, Fiat Auto, the industry laughingstock, had returned to profitability. They did this by bringing out three hot new car models in record time. One of them was the Fiat 500. They made a whimsical celebratory video they called *Carmageddon*, a play on the biblical word "Armageddon," in which they showed what trouble the company was in and how bleak the prospects were. They showed the magazine with the upside-down Fiat and all the pronouncements of death for the company. It showed how they turned it all around and then spelled out the work they still had to do. The last thing the video said was "Good news, kids, you've earned a ten-minute break, now get back to work."[80]

That was part one of the story. Marchionne still had to convince investors he was on the right track. He had to stop the losses and change the corporate culture at its roots. He had to extricate Fiat from its partnership with

GM, which would free up a lot of money. On top of all that, he had to extend the life of the $3 billion loan Fiat had taken from eight different banks and fend off the power those banks had to liquidate Fiat to get their money back. Then he had to fend off a hostile takeover.

When the downturn in 2008 happened, Fiat needed to find a partner in order to survive. Sergio and Fiat found that partner in Chrysler—but then had to find a way to save Chrysler!

Chrysler was facing bankruptcy. Long gone was the turnaround Iacocca engineered in the 1980s. The Daimler-Chrysler experiment was over, and Mercedes-Benz had sold Chrysler in 2007 to a private firm named Cerberus Capital Management, which basically ran it into the ground. The US government wouldn't extend Troubled Asset Relief Program (TARP) dollars to Chrysler if they didn't find a viable partner to help it survive the downturn.

Of all the companies in the world, Fiat was the only interested candidate. Clark writes, "The idea that Fiat, a second-tier automaker that specialized in small cars, could not only fix Chrysler's problems, but also somehow turn two weak automakers into a global competitor was audacious."

Marchionne was interested in Chrysler because of Fiat's lack of scale and its access to the US market. Chrysler was interested in Fiat because Chrysler was basically screaming for help. It was as if they needed citizenship, and if they didn't marry Fiat, they would get kicked out of the country.

On one side of the table sat the United Auto Workers and the US government, and on the other sat Sergio Marchionne.

Fiat wasn't going to put any money whatsoever into the deal. Sergio demanded 35 percent ownership of Chrysler for free. When the talks had almost broken down and the UAW and Cerberus were about to walk away, Marchionne said, "Look, this thing is broken. The only thing you can do with it is dismantle it and sell off the cars in the lot for a discount." Sergio had boldness, tenacity, and vision. "There is one person who can fix it, and he is talking to you now, and he's telling you, I am not paying cash. I can fix it, but it's unfair to pay." He stood his ground.

They said they wanted him to have "skin in the game" so he wouldn't just acquire the company and not fix it. He responded, "I don't want to talk about skin in the game. Me and my people are going to move over to Detroit and pour our lifeblood into the company. Take it or leave it."[81]

His own executives thought he should leave Chrysler for dead. UAW and Cerberus thought they had no other options. They couldn't see how it could be done. Sergio saw how to fix it, though. In the end, US taxpayers loaned Chrysler $11.2 billion to keep running, and Marchionne moved in to work.

He quickly unveiled a twenty-five-member management team, twenty-two of which were from Chrysler. He did his interviews, flattened the bureaucracy, gathered the leaders, and got the right people on the bus. It was déjà vu all over again.

Symbolically, Marchionne refused to move into the executive office suite at the top of the Chrysler building, the second largest building on the planet behind the Pentagon. He moved down to the fourth floor in a little room off to one side in what is called the banana wing. Many of the engineers and the design center are in that wing. He showed them with this move that he was just one of them. Part of the team.

Clark writes, "The clever part of this organization was it made each manager beholden to the others for their success. They were forced to work together."[82] Marchionne's unusual ability is he can see what actually needs to be done, and then he cajoles and goads his flat management structure to achieve the goal. He won't let up until it's done and won't take no for an answer. He accepts no excuses and is excellent at strategy and execution.

Chrysler came out with sixteen new models in just fourteen months. They emerged from bankruptcy and paid back the government loan, and Chrysler and Fiat were now one company spanning two continents.

During the 2011 Super Bowl a commercial featured a black car driving through a tunnel. You could see just parts of the car, and then brief flashes of the driver. Soon it became clear the driver was the rap star Eminem, and the car was the new Chrysler 200. The song playing was an Eminem song that had been requested and denied for commercials more than a hundred times. Eminem, taken with the Chrysler comeback story and a supporter of the City of Detroit, had decided not only to let them use the song but to appear in the commercial. At the end of the ad it said, "Imported from Detroit."

This was one of the top Super Bowl commercials ever, and it marked the return of Chrysler as a viable force in the auto industry. It signified a happy and unusual marriage between an Italian and a Michigander. Most important, it symbolized a legendary turnaround engineered by a remarkable leader.

MINDSET MEMOS

1. Talent often shows up early.

However, it might be underutilized until a person finds his footing, as Marchionne did in his thirties.

2. It may take several wrong turns before talent find its destiny.

Marchionne didn't fall right into the business that would become his legacy. There were some missteps and detours along the way.

3. Talent requires seasoning and education.

This is not necessarily formal education, though for Marchionne that was a large part of it. Talent needs to be nurtured and developed before it becomes fully effective toward success.

4. Roots are important.

Marchionne definitely inherited some of his mother's resilience and toughness. His parents lived in turbulent times, and the grit that got them through seemed to become a part of his leadership style.

5. Opportunities will come, eventually, for those who are prepared.

No one could have asked Marchionne twenty years ago where he would be today and received an answer anywhere close to what actually occurred.

When you strategize a game plan and look toward the future, the further out you go, the less valuable it is. You may not know where you'll be and what you'll be doing twenty years from now. But you can still prepare to be in a good place. You can do today what twenty years from now you'll wish you *had* done today.

6. Excellence polarizes.

You can't please everyone. Figure out what is right. Figure out what your instinct tells you is the thing to do and what God wants of you, and then go for it. Stand firm in your conviction, and be excellent. Then don't worry about what anybody else is saying.

7. In a world of managers, leaders are really what are needed.

When a real leader shows up, it's like a breath of fresh air. Sales will follow.

204 | MINDSET MEMOS

8. Load the right people on the bus.

John Wooden, the famous basketball coach, said there are only two things you have to do to win as a coach. You've got to find the right people, and you've got to get the most out of them. Don't drag the wrong people around. Cut them loose, and find rascals who want to win.

9. Real leaders surround themselves with other leaders.

Don't work with yes-men. Find people who will help you by challenging you. The most productive people are not always the easiest to work with. Find leaders who aren't afraid to tell you what they think.

10. Long odds are rocket fuel to a leader.

Leaders thrive on challenges. They turn expert criticism into the symbol of their next victory.

11. Vision.

Leonardo da Vinci called this *sapere vedere*, meaning "being able to see." In order to lead where no one has ever been, you need to see further. You need to get a clear vision of where you are going.

12. When you are right and you are sure, stand firm.

Marchionne didn't blink when he was negotiating the Chrysler deal. He was right, and it was a win–win.

13. Be good at both strategy and execution.

You can't be good at aiming only; you also have to fire. You also can't fire unless you know how to aim. It takes both theory and practice to make things happen. Marchionne knew how to make quality decisions quickly and then get them put immediately into action.

14. Celebrate your victories, but move on quickly.

There is always more to do. Don't rest on your laurels. Perhaps your greatest victory is ahead. You've earned a ten-minute break. Now get back to work!

NOTES

Chapter 1

1   Ingrassia, Paul. *Engines of Change: A History of the American Dream in Fifteen Cars*. New York: Simon & Schuster, 2012. Print.

2   Ibid.

3   Ibid.

Chapter 2

4   Sharp, Ken, Paul Stanley, and Gene Simmons. *Nothing to Lose: The Making of KISS 1972-1975*. Harper Collins. 2013. Print

5   Ibid.

6   Ibid.

7   Ibid.

8   Ibid.

9   Ibid.

10   Ibid.

11   Ibid.

12   Ibid.

13   Ibid.

14   Ibid.

15   Ibid.

16   Ibid.

17   Leaf, David and Ken Sharp. *KISS: Behind the Mask*. Grand Central Publishing, 2008. Print.

Chapter 3

18   Ibid.

19   Jackley, Jessica. *Clay Water Brick: Finding Inspiration From Entrepreneurs Who Do the Most With the Least*. New York: Spiegel and Grau, 2015. Print.

20   Ibid.

21   Ibid.

22   Ibid.

23   Ibid.

24   Ibid.

25   Ibid.

26   Ibid.

27   Ibid.

28   Ibid.

29   Ibid.

Chapter 4

30   Springveld, Tom. "14 Classic Johann Cruyff Quotes Explained." *Isle of Holland* 25 Feb. 2015. Online. http://isleofholland.com/read/sports/14-classic-johan-cruyff-quotes-explained

31   Kuper, Simon, and Stefan Szymanski. *Soccernomics: Why Transfers Fail, Why Spain Rule the World and Other Curious Football Phenomena Explained*. Updated ed. Print.

32   Ibid.

33   Baer, Drake. "Elon Musk Uses This Ancient Critical-Thinking Strategy to Outsmart Everybody Else." *Business*

Insider 5 Jan. 2015. Online. http://www.businessinsider.com/elon-musk-first-principles-2015-1

34   Anderson, Chris. "Elon's Mission to Mars." *Wired* 21 Oct. 2012. Online. http://www.wired.com/2012/10/ff-elon-musk-qa/

Chapter 5

35   Parrish, Charlie. "Instagram's Kevin Systrom: 'I'm dangerous enough to code and sociable enough to sell our company.'" *The Telegraph* 1 May 2015. Online. http://www.telegraph.co.uk/technology/11568119/Instagrams-Kevin-Systrom-Im-dangerous-enough-to-code-and-sociable-enough-to-sell-our-company.html

Chapter 6

36   "Bezos on Innovation." *Bloomberg Business* 16 April 2008. Online.   http://www.bloomberg.com/bw/stories/2008-04-16/bezos-on-innovation

37   Stone, Brad. *The Everything Store: Jeff Bezos and the Age of Amazon*. New York, N.Y.: Little Brown, *2013*.

38   Ibid.

39   Ibid.

40   Ibid.

41   Ibid.

42   George, Bill. "Developing Innovative Leaders." 2012. Online. http://www.billgeorge.org/page/developing-innovative-leaders

43   Stone, Brad. *The Everything Store: Jeff Bezos and the Age of Amazon*. New York, N.Y.: Little Brown, 2013.

Chapter 7

44   Witzenburg, Gary. "The Ghost: Ponycar and minivan creator talks about Ford, Iacocca, and taking risks." *Motor Trend* 26 Jan. 2013.

Online. http://www.motortrend.com/classic/features/12q1_hal_sperlich_interview/viewall.html

45   Ingrassia, Paul. *Engines of Change: A History of the American Dream in Fifteen Cars*. New York: Simon & Schuster, 2012. Print.

46   Ibid.

47   Ibid.

48   Ibid.

6   Ibid

7   Stone, Brady. "The Everything Store: Jeff Bezos and the Age of Amazon", Little, Brown and Company, NY, 2013

Chapter 8

49   http://www.art-quotes.com/auth_search.php?authid=6230#.VgoXavlViko

50   Kuskey, G. Eric, and Bettina Gilois. *Billion Dollar Painter: The Triumph and Tragedy of Thomas Kinkade, Painter of Light*. Print.

51   Ibid.

52   Ibid.

53   Ibid.

54   Ibid.

55   Ibid.

Chapter 9

56   Brunner, Robert, and Stewart Emery. *Do You Matter? How Great Design Will Make People Love Your Company*. Upper Saddle River, N.J.: FT, 2009. Print.

57   Kahney, Leander. *Jony Ive: The Genius behind Apple's Greatest Products*. Penguin Group, 2013. Print.

58   Ibid.

59   Ibid.

60   Ibid.

61   Ibid.

62   Isaacson, Walter. *Steve Jobs*. New York: Simon & Schuster, 2011. Print.

63   Kahney, Leander. *Jony Ive: The Genius Behind Apple's Greatest Products*. Penguin Group, 2013. Print.

64   Ibid.

65   Ibid.

66   Isaacson, Walter. *Steve Jobs*. New York: Simon & Schuster, 2011. Print.

67   Kahney, Leander. *Jony Ive: The Genius behind Apple's Greatest Products*. Penguin Group, 2013. Print.

68   Ibid.

69   Ibid.

70   Ibid.

71   Ibid.

Chapter 10

Baer, Drake. "Elon Musk Uses This Ancient Critical-Thinking Strategy to Outsmart Everybody Else." *Business Insider* 5 Jan. 2015. Online. http://www.businessinsider.com/elon-musk-first-principles-2015-1

Anderson, Chris. "Elon's Mission to Mars." *Wired* 21 Oct. 2012. Online. http://www.wired.com/2012/10/ff-elon-musk-qa/

Chapter 11

72   Ingrassia, Paul. "Resurrecting Chrysler." *Wall Street Journal* 3 July 2010. Online. http://www.wsj.com/articles/SB100014240527487 04198004575311051465765446

212 | MINDSET MEMOS

73   Clark, Jennifer. *Mondo Agnelli Fiat, Chrysler, and the Power of a Dynasty*. Hoboken, NJ: John Wiley & Sons, 2012. Print.

74   Ibid.

75   Ibid.

76   Ibid.

77   Ibid.

78   Ibid.

79   Ibid.

80   Ibid.

81   Ibid.

82   Ibid.

FINANCIAL FITNESS PROGRAM

You've Worked Enough for Money,
Now It's Time to Get It Working for You!

FREE PERSONAL WEBSITE

SIGN UP AND TAKE ADVANTAGE OF THESE FREE FEATURES:

- Personal website
- Take your custom assessment test
- Build your own profile
- Share milestones and successes with partners and friends
- Post videos and photos
- Receive daily info "nuggets"

FINANCIAL FITNESS BASIC PROGRAM

The first program to teach all three aspects of personal finance: defense, offense, and playing field. Learn the simple, easy-to-apply principles that can help you shore up your resources, get out of debt, and build stability for a more secure future. It's all here, including a comprehensive book, companion workbook, and 8 audios that amplify the teachings from the books.

Also available DIGITALLY!

financialfitnessinfo.com

FINANCIAL FITNESS
MASTER CLASS

Buy it once and use it forever! Designed to provide a continual follow-up to the principles learned in the Basic Program, this ongoing educational support offers over 6 hours of video and over 14 hours of audio instruction that walk you through the workbook, step by step. Perfect for individual or group study.
6 videos, 15 audios

FINANCIAL FITNESS
TRACK AND SAVE

The Financial Fitness Program teaches you how to get out of debt, build additional streams of income, and properly take advantage of tax deductions. Now, with this subscription, we give you the tools to do so. The Tracker offers mobile expense tracking tools and budgeting software, while the Saver offers you thousands of coupons and discounts to help you save money every day.

THE WEALTH HABITS SERIES

The Wealth Habits series is designed to help you prosper through consistent, ongoing, simple, and enjoyable financial literacy education. You will learn timeless principles about how to better handle your money, and timely commentary on the current economic forces affecting the "playing field" upon which we all must participate. Small doses of information applied consistently over time can produce enormous results through the formation of new and profitable habits. This is what the Wealth Habits series is all about.

WEALTHABITS
SERIES

The Wealth Habits series will put you in a unique position. You will know something that only a few people in the world know. You will know the principles of financial fitness. You have the power to not only develop financial fitness but also to positively impact the lives of those around you. And the time to act is NOW.

LEARN TO NOT ONLY *SURVIVE*, BUT *THRIVE* DURING TOUGH ECONOMIC TIMES!

BEYOND FINANCIAL FITNESS PROGRAM

The original Financial Fitness program taught all three aspects of personal finance:defense, offense, and playing field. Now, the long anticipated Beyond Financial Fitness builds on that platform by teaching how to maximize the potential of your various streams of income by properly accumulating an ever-growing portfolio of cash-flow-producing assets.

Drawn from many of the greatest minds in the history of personal finance, the Beyond Financial Fitness program teaches you to gain mastery over your money once and for all and includes a comprehensive book, audio version of the book, a companion workbook, 4 audios, and 2 DVDs. Bookmark and decal also included. *You've worked enough for money, now it's time to get it working for you!*

Also available DIGITALLY!

financialfitnessinfo.com